This Too Shall Pass

by
LaBelle Lance
with Gary Sledge

CHRISTIAN HERALD BOOKS
Chappaqua, NY 10514

We acknowledge with appreciation permission to reprint brief passages from:

The New York Times
The Washington Post
The Atlanta Constitution

*This book
is dedicated to
the Glory of God
through his Son
Jesus Christ*

Prologue

This too shall pass. Slowly, or all too quickly, agonizingly, joyfully, or sadly—time passes. The sun rises and sets. We grow older. Lives change. And hopefully we grow wiser, more patient, more loving.

Our family has been through every kind of trial. My mother says that if you live long enough you will taste a bit of everything: hate and love, joy and sorrow, tragedy and ecstasy, beauty and ugliness. Let me just list the human afflictions that have touched my life: alcoholism, drugs, broken homes, suicide, death, violence, serious illness, car accidents, jailings, homosexuality, murder, adultery, runaway children. Everything that suffering flesh can feel. But suffering teaches, and life goes on. We endure. We persevere. Because there is no other way. We do what we have to do. Take what we have to take—a day at a time. There is only one way to look for strength—up, to God. We must learn to pray without ceasing, making God uppermost in our thoughts. We will feel his hands holding our lives. We are nothing without him, only empty vessels to be molded and filled.

People frequently asked me, "Do you think the press was fair to you?" I don't think so. But I don't blame them. Is life fair? We have been blessed and we have had to suffer. Both come from the hand of God who works all things for the good. And I have learned this: our nation is great because all her institutions, human and fallible though they be—from the Presidency to the press—try to live up to the biblical and democratic principles on which they are founded. We all must guard against the baser instincts in public life—false accusations and pleasure in another's distress—but I trust that my story will show the vibrancy of life rather than the evil. Because we are covered with the armor of God—his salvation—we can live life with grace and joy. If we trust and obey him, he will guide us through the days of darkness to the light and love which is Jesus Christ.

Our family is not so different from any other. But I'd like you to walk with me down the Lance road of life, if only to illustrate how wonderful is the Lord on whom we rely. Everyone of us needs someone. Life is too hard to take alone. Should we not turn to the only one who will never leave or forsake us? Friends and family pass on, but God is always there.

—LaBelle Lance
Calhoun, GA
January, 1978

Washington
Resignation Day

Laughter and many loud voices and the sound of shuffling feet. I started up out of a fitful sleep, realizing that they were there outside the house again.

"Good morning, darling," Bert said, easing me out of troubled half-consciousness. He placed a breakfast tray with a fresh rose on my bedside table. "Good morning," I sleepily replied. I glanced at the glowing red digits on the bedside clock: 6:25. Time for Bert to leave for the office. The laughter and commotion continued in the street below. They were waiting for Bert.

Georgetown is ordinarily one of the nice quiet residential districts of Washington. For that reason, and because it was only a short ride to Bert's office across the street from the White House, we decided to rent here when President Carter asked Bert to join the Cabinet as Director of the Office of Management and Budget. Today was different. Our quiet street was buzzing again with traffic. We were under seige, as we had been thoughout September. Today was September 21.

For weeks newspaper reporters, TV crews and other newsmen had been camping on our front doorstep. Our bedroom was on the second floor in the front of our red brick townhouse. In recent days the crowd formed out on the sidewalk under our window before daybreak. The reporters and newscasters had come to realize that Bert got up very early, and they would first try to catch him when he went out the front door to get the morning paper. Bert would always open the door, give them a cheerful wave, pick up *The Post*

and come back inside. Then they would wait for him to leave
for work. He would then run a gauntlet of reporters shouting questions and bristling with microphones and note-
books. Most followed him down to the Executive Office
Building, but a few would stay and occasionally come up to
ring the doorbell to ask me questions. By noon most would
drift away, leaving their coffee cups and film packs in the
gutter. I wondered what the neighbors must think of this
whole morning scene. The last couple of days the sidewalk
had been more crowded than usual because speculation
was rampant that Bert's resignation was imminent now that
he had presented his case to the Senate Committee and
answered their probing questions.

Bert's routine was to get up around 5:30 and have coffee
by himself. That's always been his quiet time, a time to be
alone with his thoughts and his Lord. He used that hour to
think, organize what he would do for the day, and spend
some time in personal prayer and meditation. When we first
moved to Washington, he had really enjoyed the quietness
of the city's dawns before his nonstop business day began. I
let him have this time alone, by himself. Even if I awoke, I
would stay in bed while he got ready for his day at the office.

Before he left, Bert always brought me up a breakfast tray
with coffee, cereal or a sweet roll, and orange juice. There
was a small camellia garden in the rear of the townhouse and
a rose garden in the front. If a camellia or a rose were in
bloom, Bert would pick one for me and put it on the breakfast tray. This morning's rose was small and fragrant. I would
keep the flower on my writing table to remind me of him and
his thoughtfulness.

Years before, when Bert started working as head of the
Georgia Highway Department, he got up unusually early to
commute seventy miles from Calhoun to Atlanta. And since
he was away so long each day, he also began the practice of
leaving a little note for me beside the flower. He'd write
something nice—perhaps recalling a recent incident or
comment, perhaps telling me that I had looked pretty at a
party the night before. Then he'd also tell me about his plans

for the day. Or if times had been hard, he'd give me a word of encouragement.

In Washington he usually left for the office about 6:30. He'd leave the morning paper on the bed, quietly kiss me good-bye and leave for the office. I'd get up then and the tray would be waiting. A little coffeepot was ready to plug in and perk.

This particular morning I dreaded the idea of looking at the paper; recently there had been a story on the front page of *The Post* about my brother Banks' death two years before. The writer implied that our family's financial situation was rocky, that Bert was somehow responsible, and that this was the reason my brother had taken his own life. All that was untrue. That article hurt me more than anything else I had read or endured during the long hot summer of allegations, inquiry and trial by public opinion. I loved my husband and my brother. I knew them as I knew my own soul; I knew their integrity, their strengths, their weaknesses, their goodness, and their friendship for one another. My brother was a good person. A loving man. A man who required nothing but the best from himself, but imperfection weighed heavily on him. He was sensitive and the harsh edges of life hurt him.

My brother Banks was a fine man, a sinner as we all are, but a good and decent human being. But a man who put great pressures on himself, set very high standards. If he could have lived a halfway life, or life in a sleepwalk, as so many of us do, he could have survived. But his goals and ideals were the highest, the best. And he felt all too keenly the buffeting of life. When his high expectations for himself were not realized, he felt unreasonable guilt or failure. He couldn't accept forgiveness from God in order to begin again.

Nothing is unforgivable with Christ. My brother's guilt and failures, I know, are washed away, even as I pray mine will be. No one comes too late to God, not even the thief on the cross who, in his dying breath, acknowledged Jesus as the Son of God. That is scripture that I want to claim. I know life is unfair. I have been greatly blessed, but I have also been and will continue to be greatly tested. I pray to God that I will witness to his glory in all circumstances and be as tolerant and forgiving of others as Christ is of me. I know my Lord accepts us, sinners though we all are—I wish we could accept ourselves as well. I wish we could accept others with his love and forgiveness. But we are hard on ourselves and hard on others. And the news of Banks' death was unnaturally hard on me.

That article broke my strength. I sat on the bed that morning too stunned to cry. It seemed so unreal, so unfair. How could they say this? Why would someone print something that would obviously hurt my mother and my brother's wife and little girls so much—just to get at Bert.

When I talked with Bert on the phone later that morning, I shared the hurt I felt and said, "Darling, I really wonder if it's worth it after all." It was the first time I had even hinted at the possibility I might agree to Bert's resigning.

Later that afternoon Bert played tennis with President Carter. When he came home, late in the afternoon, he looked exhausted. I had planned a candlelight dinner for us out on our little patio behind the house. I knew that he'd be in the mood for a quiet dinner for just the two of us. He put his briefcase down by the white and yellow ribbon-striped Chippendale sofa in the living room, and walked tiredly toward the patio, but then he sat down on a lounge chair in our little garden room just off the patio.

"The President and I had a little discussion this afternoon," he said. He paused and looked at me—as if he had something more to say.

I felt a moment of panic.

"I've done a lot of thinking—I've prayed about it. It may be best that I resign now and go back home. We could get our business in order and our names wouldn't be on the front page every day. I don't mind for myself; I can take that. I'll stand up for anything I've said or done. But when they keep on hurting my family . . . well, it's not worth it."

I could see the suppressed anger in his face, the tiredness and the letting go. I knelt beside him and took his hand. I didn't want him to give up! Not for me; not for anyone. I would stand by him, hold him up if he needed any support. I wouldn't let my emotional burden drag him down. We had come to Washington so bright and full of hope, so eager to do a job, so anxious to do what we felt God wanted us to do. He was still needed here by the President and the people. He hadn't done anything to warrant this.

Then at supper in the garden, we asked God to give us wisdom and strength and to show us his will as we said a blessing over the simple meal I'd prepared. Prayer is not what we turn to as a last resort; it is our first recourse, our primary resource. We were brought up that way. God was not far off. He was near. We talked to him intimately and often. We had learned to call him and to praise him on all occasions. I gazed up at Bert and saw his dear, familiar face cast in flickering light and shadow from the candles. A breath of wind brought the fragrance of the flowers to me. "Nothing can happen that will really hurt us," I thought. "Nothing can change the love we have for one another."

Today would tell the tale. We had prayed and Bert had slept on it once again. Now he'd gone off to the White House. The note beside the rose on the tray said only, "My dearest, I love you, LaBelle. Will call later—Bert."

Outside I heard the scuffling, the talk, and the laughter as they took down the cameras and the sound equipment.

Our days in Washington had been the busiest, most exciting, weightiest of our lives. Washington is a place of powerful people and great stress—a place of power, ambition, public adulation and condemnation. It is a showcase for people, a winepress of personalities and power. The feeling that you are at the center of great events, that you are playing a part that you desire, a part that will help strengthen this nation, is exciting and gratifying. It takes prayer to keep your feet on the ground and a proper perspective on life. But—isn't this true wherever we live? Washington is like every other place or situation—it offers an opportunity for service and witness, or it can become a trap of temptation, indulgence and pride.

But at long last our long summer trial was drawing to an end, I thought. Bert, according to virtually all news media, had accounted himself very well at the Senate hearings. I knew he had! As he told me later, it was as if he had been surrounded by a ring of fire in peace and serenity and the truth of God. It showed. God gives strength sufficient to our trials and our needs. Now Bert, I had hoped, would be able to get on with his job. I could get on with my living and helping him. But then yesterday's quick reversal of our mood ... the newspaper story about my brother's tragic death and Bert's talk with the President.

I lay in bed until I no longer heard the voices of the newsmen out in the street. Then I picked up the breakfast tray resting on the bedside table and plugged in the little coffeepot. Bert's note and the rose still lay next to the pot. In a minute, I poured a cup, took a sip, and tried to collect my thoughts.

What should I do? I wondered. Do I have any choice? Is this something solely between the President and my husband? Are political factors and forces the sole and overriding considerations? Do my feelings count when matters of national significance are being shaped? Was it true that the government's and public's attention was so occupied with the "Lance Affair" that nothing was getting done? Surely our government was large enough, even bureaucratic enough to muddle through while Bert worked out his solution. And what kind of system of Cabinet-level examination was it that proceeded by invective, innuendo and a hunger for personal destruction? Bert had not acted irresponsibly as was being said—his board of directors at the bank, his fellow workers and bankers, his fellow townspeople were completely behind him. Weren't these the very people who would have been hurt most by his actions?

My mind wandered aimlessly over all the problems that had plagued me for weeks. I was at a loss, unable to sort out the issues, unable to place responsibility for our state of affairs. But I was sure of two essential things: my love for my husband, and his innocence. I was confident that God still had a plan for us, that he was bringing the result he wanted out of our muddled human affairs.

But how hard it is for us to figure out. Lean not on your own understanding, but the Lord's, I told myself. I finished breakfast in bed. At 8:30 A.M. my son Tram called from Atlanta.

Tram, David, Stuart and Beverly had all been very thoughtful and considerate throughout the long days of summer and the Senate hearings. The boys called regularly just to say "hello," and to make sure that I was all right with each new onslaught of news in the media. It's great to see your children grow up and take on responsibility for themselves and their own families. It's great to see their concern and support for each other. Tram, who had given us occasions for worry, as do the children of all parents, was now fretting about his little boy's colic and whether he was eating properly. He was being drawn out of himself, as we all are, by an infant's vulnerability and innocence. Every time I looked at my grandson, I thought, this is how Jesus wants us to come to him, vulnerable but trusting, full of needs and demands on him, but as guileless and innocent as a little child.

How often we make things more complicated than they really are. How hard it is to learn to rely on God to do for us what we cannot do ourselves—as a child learns to trust and rely on his parents to open a door, or tie his shoes, or lift him up high to reach the unreachable.

Now Tram was concerned about us. How were we bearing up? He was aware of the escalation of the media's stories and reports about Bert's impending resignation. He was worried about me, because he had seen the article written about my brother and he knew I would be upset.

"Momma, are you all right?" he asked. He must have heard the tension in my voice.

I told him about his daddy's tennis game with the President and what his attitude had been last night—and that I wasn't sure if he had determined to stay or quit. But, I told him, I was still positively opposed to resignation.

"What are you going to do, Momma?" he asked. "I think you should call the President right now."

"Do you really think so, Tram? I'm not sure," I said. "I feel I should call. I don't want your daddy to resign because he thinks there's too much pressure on me and the family. We wouldn't be bearing our share of the load if he did that. We have to carry our share and support him as he would support us. And I don't want him to resign just because he thinks the President might want him to. I know the President wants men around him who stand on their own two feet, and stand up for the country."

"Does the President know how you feel about it?"

"I think Daddy told him I had a sinking spell, a deep sadness. He is questioning whether it is worth it. I wondered that too, when the story about your Uncle Banks came out yesterday. Maybe I should let the President know that I'm still against Daddy's leaving."

We talked on for a few more minutes debating the situation, sharing our emotions, each of us eager for understanding from one another. When we finally hung up, I was still uncertain. Then, all of a sudden, I picked up the phone which had the direct line to the White House and heard myself asking the switchboard operator for Susan Clough, the President's personal secretary. Immediately I had second thoughts. Should I be bothering the President with my personal feelings? The phone rang and then Susan was on the line.

"Hello, Susan, this is LaBelle Lance," I heard myself calmly saying. "I know the President is very busy, but if he has a moment sometime this morning I'd really like to talk to him about something on my heart. It's pretty important."

She told me that he was then in conference with a foreign minister, but she would give him the message. I thanked her and hung up. Well, I'd done it.

When I'm anxious I like to get busy. Work soothes the soul. So I went into the kitchen and cleaned up from breakfast, then I vacuumed the living room, put some clothes in the washer, and started getting ready for lunch. After a while I heard the front door open, and glanced at the kitchen clock. It was only 10:30. I hadn't expected Bert home until at least noon. He put his briefcase down by the hall bench as I came out to meet him.

"You're early," was all I could say, wondering what that might mean.

"I've decided I'm going to resign," he said. "I saw the President first thing this morning."

"But I have a call in for him now. I was going to tell him I'm against it. And I am, Bert. I want you to stay. Public opinion is going with you now. Thousands of people have been praying for you. It's going to work out."

"I know it's hard for you," he said. "It's hard for me. I had a dream about what could be accomplished in this job. But it is the right thing to do."

"I don't think so," I said. "The political reasons don't concern me. I'm for you and for whatever is God's will. Nothing has led me to believe that God wants us to leave."

"If I get Clark Clifford to talk to you, would that convince you?"

Can it be all over, I wondered? Somehow I didn't think so. Bert called Clark Clifford. He was at a meeting in Detroit and would call back. All this time I was rushing around making sandwiches, though neither one of us was hungry. We ate and talked. Then just as we got up from the table, the President called back. Bert answered and talked with him a minute and then handed it to me saying, "Jimmy's returning your call."

The President was very cordial, very gracious. He invited me to come to the White House and talk with him. He likes to tease me and jokingly he said that he always liked to talk to a pretty lady. I'm sure he was trying his best to put me at ease. He always is a friend to everyone in our family on a person-to-person basis, despite the formalities of his office. I think the President believes strongly that Christ's love and concern can only be shown in this way.

I laughed and told him I always loved seeing my President.

It was then about 12:30 and he asked us to come at 1:15. I had on slacks and I wanted to change, so quickly I ran upstairs. Clark Clifford, Bert's lawyer during the Senate hearings, called while I was dressing and Bert told him that he had decided to resign, but that I was against it. Clark said he would return to Washington on an early plane to help in whatever way he could. Bert left then to go to the Executive Office Building. He was to see the President before his news conference scheduled for 3:00. He would meet me at the side entrance of the White House at 1:15.

I had quickly dressed. I got my pocketbook and was ready to go; Bert had called someone from his office to drive me to the White House. As we were traveling across town, it occurred to me suddenly how appropriate was the biblical metaphor describing politics as a sea. That image certainly captured the vastness, the tempestuousness, the power, the ups and downs, the loneliness of political life.

When the car got to the White House, the guard glanced up at me and knowing me well waved us in through the black wrought-iron gates. Bert was not waiting outside.

I got out of the car and walked up the steps to the office-side entrance of the White House. It always gave me a deep sense of pride to be here. Each wife of a Cabinet Officer has a White House pass. I had been there many times, but I still felt a special sense of privilege being there. I walked up the corridor and turned toward the Oval Office. Bert was waiting in the hall outside and in a moment the President came to the open door and invited us in. The Oval Office is very beautiful with its light-colored oval rug and eggshell-white walls. The gold draperies frame three windows behind the President's large, dark carved desk. There by the windows stand the American and the Presidential flags. The grace and the formality of the 18th-century furniture, including traditional wing chairs by the fireplace, is most appropriate for state business. Two striped sofas face each other across a butler's table. The President guided us along to the smaller office beyond the Oval Office, which is his personal work area and a more intimate place to meet. It is cozier and more private.

There was a sofa against the wall on one side of his desk. Bert and I sat there together. There are small paintings and

family photographs in the room. The President keeps me-
mentoes on his desk. I tried to collect my thoughts, and
when the President asked me how I felt, I outlined my
position.

Bert was doing a good job in his office, I said, and now
that the Senate hearings were over, the press' attention
would shift and he could move forward in his job. He and
the President are friends, loyal to one another. Bert would be
a strong team member to help push forward the Administration's goals. And I told the President that I had sought God's
will and wisdom in prayer, and I believed that Bert should
not resign.

The President listened and seriously considered all that I
said. He asked me some questions. He spoke honestly about
his public relations problem caused by Bert's name being in
the news so long. He said that later in the afternoon he was
scheduled to have a news conference and that there were
top-priority programs and legislation he wanted to talk
about. He mentioned his proposed treaty concerning the
Panama Canal in particular. He felt the American people
needed to hear about these issues. But he said that when he
opened the floor to questions, eight out of ten questions
would probably be about Bert's situation. He said that Bert
knew this and had decided, for both political and personal
reasons, to resign.

I knew that the President had presented his views in the
light of faith. He, just as Bert and I, had prayed about this
situation and each of us reached different conclusions—but
each of us had come to realize the profound love in Christ we
shared. I was convinced I was speaking the word God
wanted me to say, the reasons and the outcome would be
His. Of course I have often learned God's purpose and my
intentions are not always the same. Yet everything comes in
his own time! Neither the President nor I knew that our
personal view was ultimately right, yet both of us were
certain that God guided each of us to reach decisions that
would affect the future for the best. We were all convinced
that all things, in Christ, work together for good.

I guess I was the first to rise. I thanked the President.

"I appreciate the opportunity to talk with you," I said. "You know I love you both very much." And I put my hand on his arm and said, "You know I'll always pray for you."

He smiled and nodded, and I sensed the profound emotions he must have felt and the various forces that come to bear on the man who holds his office. What an awesome, deep responsibility he has. We shook hands, and Bert and I left and went to the Cabinet Room down the hall from the Oval Office to be alone for a minute. Bert took a yellow lined sheet of legal paper out of his pocket and spread it on the table.

"I've been writing a letter of resignation. I'd like you to read it and work with me on it."

· But my emotions were welling up in me again.

"I can't. I'm still against it." I said. "It's one thing I can't help you with. I don't really want to see it. If you feel that it's something you must do, you'll have to do it alone." I was suddenly tired. So many months, so many plans, so much personal travail—all to come to this. Would he actually resign? I was still hoping he would not. Perhaps both he and the President would still change their minds. I thought it was best for me to go home. I kissed him and left him standing by the chair that had been his as an officer in the Cabinet of the United States.

I left the White House at about 2:15 and was driven home. Bert went across the street to the Executive Office Building after he finished his statement. I rode through the streets that should have seemed familiar, but Washington never seemed stranger. What a huge, complicated city full of entanglements, aspirations, strengths and weaknesses. I found myself back at our front door with no consciousness of intervening time. I unlocked the door, went inside, and turned on the TV to wait for the President's news conference, but it had been postponed two hours until 5:00. What now, I wondered. Is Bert still working on his letter? Has the President changed his mind? Has Clark Clifford intervened at the last minute, counseling Bert and the President to wait? Tram called again.

"What in the world's going on?" he asked. "The Atlanta

station said the President's conference will be delayed for an hour or two—and they expect to have Daddy's resignation."

By the time I hung up the phone, the reporters were gathering again in the street. Someone came up and rang the doorbell. They knew it was my policy always to answer the door—I believe that Jesus requires that. My commitment is to try always to greet people and keep open the door of my house. God sends all kinds to the door. I try to receive each as if he were Jesus.

The bell rang again before I could get there, and then someone stuffed a note through the mail slot. So I picked it up off the floor. Some reporter just wanted to know when Bert would be home—and I didn't know myself. I stood inside the door, listening to the growing volume of voices, and hesitated, and then finally opened the door halfway. There was a man on the first landing talking down toward a directional microphone while the technician took readings. He looked surprised to see me in the doorway.

"Tell them Bert should be home pretty soon, but I don't know when. I'll visit with you later," I said, because several had asked me for a statement when I came back from the White House. I closed the door again on his startled look.

Sometimes my open door policy had been misinterpreted. A couple of times I had gone to the door dressed in slacks and a bit rumpled from doing housework and the next day I'd read that "Mrs. Lance was seen at home looking very harried." I didn't know whether to laugh or groan about this sort of thing. I just left the results up to God but I wondered what the startled man on our steps would say or write and I smiled to myself.

I went back to the TV but only the afternoon game shows were on, so I turned off the set and read a daily devotional book.

Bert came home at ten minutes to five. More reporters had followed him from the E.O.B., so the whole front walk was full again.

"I've resigned. It's all over, except what will be in the media," he told me. "I wrote this too—it's for you and the boys—to let you know what you all mean to me." And he handed me a folded yellow sheet of paper like the one on which he had written his resignation. It was a personal message of his own for us, not something I feel I want to share, but something I will always treasure.

At 5 P.M. the President's press conference came on. The President read Bert's short resignation letter, made a statement of confidence and support for Bert and began answering questions of newsmen who were still trying to find some hidden meaning or motive in the resignation and the whole affair.

Together we watched the whole news conference and it seemed that our lives had been objectified, reduced, transformed into signs, symbols, puppets—pros and cons; but where were we, where were the real people? It was so strange to hear Bert referred to in the past tense as if, passing from office, he had disappeared. Only the President's kind, brotherly words in support of Bert lifted our spirits.

As soon as the President had finished reading the statement, we started to get calls from friends, family and supporters from all over the country. We asked Jewel Miller, Bert's personal secretary to tell the White House switchboard, to intercept all calls and let only family through. I tried to reach all the children, and I hoped that they had not seen the conference or been told. Beverly, our youngest son, was out on the football field watching band practice and a friend told him before I could. I felt bad that he had to hear about it this way, and to try to understand it all without us there. But it had been so quickly done; there was no time, nor did I have any positive information to convey to the family before the news conference.

I called Clark Clifford. He explained why he thought the resignation was best. He said that Bert had made a strong presentation at the Senate hearings and that the American people were still behind him. He had hoped that Bert would be able to stay and carry on with his work, but political pressures were still operating and it might be best for Bert to go home and put his affairs in order and avoid the weltering fire of the media. I thanked him for all his help. We were supposed to go to the Cliffords' for dinner that night, but I declined saying that Bert and I needed to be alone.

The street was full of newsmen and camera crews now, and some kept knocking on the door.

"I don't want to see them now," Bert said. "I've given my statement through the President."

"Let me talk to them. I want to make a statement of faith. I promised some of them I would. I'll ask them to give us some peace now."

"Don't say anything against all this, though, and don't say anything about the President," Bert said. I promised.

So I went out, and stood on the top landing. The street was full of people. It looked like a small army. There was no pushing, shoving, or shouting. They were gentlemen. They treated me like a lady. When they saw me they quieted down. At first my heart was racing, because I knew that this might go on the air. I didn't want to lose my composure. I spoke softly, so the sound men asked me to come down to the second landing on our steps. And they thrust up their microphones on extension rods, and got their pads and pencils ready.

I told them and the nation that it was our love of Christ that had brought us through this time. I told them that we all rest on God's purpose, and that I was sure Bert and I were doing what God required of us. I said I had not wanted my husband to resign, but it was not my decision to make. And I closed with a statement of my love for God and my pride in being an American and my pride in the government of our country.

The most surprising thing was that when I had finished, they applauded. I hadn't expected that. News people don't do that. There were no shouted questions. Just applause. It brought tears to my eyes. And I went back into the house hurriedly because I didn't want them to see me crying.

They did leave us alone after that. Bert made a special omelette for dinner. And we had a glass of champagne. We weren't sad or disappointed. We wanted to celebrate quietly. We were not mourning. It was done—so it must suit God's plan. For a while we discussed plans for going home, then we went to bed early and Bert fell right asleep and slept soundly. But I lay awake for a while thinking. "It is finished," I thought. I thanked the Lord for the opportunity to come to Washington and also the opportunity to leave.

I began making plans for closing the house and moving back home to Georgia.

Calhoun

It was my granddaddy who taught me to look and listen, who taught me about love and butterflies. He and I went on long walks in the hills and fields. He took me quail hunting. He shared his love of nature with me. He showed me how God's finger touched each leaf and arranged the petals of every flower. He was my guide in so many ways.

When I was eleven my daddy taught me to ride out at "The Cabin," Granddaddy's farm three miles north of Calhoun. I loved it—the old lodge built of real logs, the meadows, springs, woods and twelve-acre lake. Many Saturday mornings while the grass was still glistening with early dew, I'd help saddle my horse, Fox, and practice my riding.

An uncle later taught me how to groom him for shows. How to brush and curry him, how to plait his mane with ribbons. But Daddy taught me timing. Learning timing was the beginning of everything, he insisted. A sense of timing, he claimed, was the essence of natural ability with a horse. Speed would come later. Timing was what put grace in motion. It was what made an eleven-year-old girl, who weighed scarcely more than her saddle, appear natural, at ease, and in command of a 1200-pound horse.

"If you keep practicing, you'll soon be taking all the ribbons," Daddy said. "Let Fox show you how." Fox belonged to the five gaited class. He was a thoroughbred and his sire had been a champion show horse. So round and round the ring I'd go—exhilarated by some fairytale image of myself with no inkling of fear.

One morning I took a bad fall. Fox was cantering. The

saddle turned, and I was dragged under the belly of the horse for perhaps a hundred feet before I fell to the ground. The next thing I remember was hearing Daddy and Grand- daddy running toward me, calling out my name. Dizzily I got up and tried to catch Fox and scramble back up. I saw the fear in their eyes, and I began to cry. "Why?" I wondered. Because they'd seen the hurt and humiliation in mine? Be- cause the shock of mortality had pushed so close? Daddy put his arm around me and took the reins from my hands and held me close for a moment.

"That's all right, honey," he said, "No broken bones. Get back on now. Otherwise you'll never get back on. That's what makes you a competitor and not just a rider."

"Give her a minute to compose herself, son," Grand- daddy said. "LaBelle, you must remount with dignity, keep your chin up and smile, even if you're crying. That's the difference between a competitor and a lady."

And I nodded and tried to smile through my tears. It was many years before I learned that a Christian is compelled by the Lord's example to follow similar advice. Nothing in this world comes easy, but we are asked to take up our cross daily, no matter how many times we falter or fall. The Lord gives us the ability to carry on, and since all time lies in his hands our spiritual walk is graceful, blessed with timing, even if our bodies or hearts are broken.

Calhoun is the one place which seems constant and sure. Its history is my history. Its people, my people.

When I sit and think of my home and my childhood, I think of Sunday morning. I see it invariably as a sunny day in May or June just when school is drawing to an eventful close. Summer still lies tantalizingly ahead. Mother helps me dress. She ties the taffeta sash behind my white cotton dress. I put on white leather slippers with a strap and buckle and appraise my appearance in the mirror hanging on the bedroom door. I smile. It's the best day of the week.

Then the front door slams and Granddaddy calls up the stairs, "Everybody ready?" He's come to take us to Sunday school. There is always a last minute rushing around, checking for purses, handkerchiefs, keys, fans. Many of the ladies in church, keeping with old southern customs, have painted silk fans. Is Daddy going today? He's not up yet. I check to make sure that I have my dime for the offering and that my bow is properly tied.

"Come on now, Grandmother," Granddaddy says, though she is the only one who's been ready all along, and has been waiting patiently just inside the front door holding her handbag in front of her.

"Was everything all right last night, Ruth?" Grandmother asks. She's always worried about Daddy.

"He was all right. Happy, not too loud. LaBelle slept right through," Mother says.

Granddaddy puts his hand behind my head and guides me out the door. We drive in Granddaddy's shiny black Packard down Wall Street past his big two-story house with the big porch and white columns to the Calhoun Methodist Church.

The adults go into the sanctuary which has the beautiful, bigger-than-life-size stained glass windows of Jesus the Good Shepherd, Jesus and the Children, and Jesus praying on the hard cold stone of the Garden of Gethsemane that I love. I go to Sunday school in the basement. There is the same musty, familiar smell—a combination of old rooms, old books, candle wax, cool musty walls and the sound of excited children's voices. There's running, noise and laughter before the teachers get everyone settled down. There are pictures everywhere. A felt-covered board on an easel tells the flannel-graph story of Jonah, which the teachers use to remind us not only of Jonah but of Christ's death and resurrection. The whale is a black football shape emerging from the blue, saw-tooth sea.

My friends, the same boys and girls I see every day in school, gather together in a large group before breaking into graded classes. The leader, Tom's mother, begins the opening "exercises" with a prayer, her clear sweet voice hushing the children. Then she tells us an object lesson, and ends with "What would Jesus want you to do in this case?" A dozen hands fly up and eagerly wave back and forth to

answer. Then in bold, bright sopranos like a flock of small
birds we energetically sing. The familiar words:

> Jesus loves me! This I know
> For the Bible tells me so;
> Little ones to him belong;
> They are weak, but He is strong.

I'm not weak, I think. I can take care of myself. And take
care of my mother. I have duties and I'm a big girl. Yet, I
know Jesus is so much stronger—stronger than my problems. God is my Father. He always listens; he never turns me
away. After a brief benediction, we all become bundles of
energy again bouncing to our separate classrooms for Bible
lessons.

I remember one class in particular. I was in the fourth
grade at the time. Our teacher, Mrs. Lang, told us about the
parable of the workers in the vineyard.

"Is it fair that everyone gets the same reward?" Mrs.
Lang asked. She had the kindest face and a loving voice.

"I don't think so," my friend Bobbie said. "The first men
worked more and they should get more."

"Is it like picking cotton?" asked Kay. "I mean, do the
workers get paid a certain amount for every pound they
pick? And the person who picks the most pounds get the
most money? That's fair."

"No. Everyone got the same. The one who picked the
most received the same pay as the one who picked the least.
The ones who came late got the same pay as the ones who
came early. In the same way God rewards with the kingdom
of heaven all those who truly believe in Christ." Mrs. Lang
said.

I listened to the whole discussion, too animated in spirit
to say anything. That was unusual for me. I had always felt
surrounded by the love of God and church. I was sure of my
faith, enfolded in the arms of a loving family. I thought of
God not as a taskmaster overseeing labor in the fields, but as
the head of my family. I had a much clearer picture in my
mind of God the loving Father than I did of Christ. With my

notion of the family of God, I suppose I couldn't yet imagine Christ as my redeemer. The story of the workers in the vineyard troubled me somewhat. In my childish way I expected heaven to be like earth, only better. Were some people to be excluded? I found that thought troubling. And I had thought that those who labored longer were to receive a richer reward.

Our class always ended with a prayer. That morning I bowed my head and silently prayed for God to watch over my little world. "Bless Granddaddy, Grandmother, Mother, Barker, Banks, and please help and watch over Daddy."

Daddy was not a church-going type. He liked "fun." He had always been given whatever he wanted. Nothing was too good for the David boys. His loving family indulged him and unconsciously they nurtured his weaknesses. I remember him in a different context. He liked to take me with him to cotton auctions, weaving mills and around to different farms and warehouses. He taught me how to grade and judge cotton—how to pick the best bales of long and short staple cotton, how to pull apart the staple to measure the quality. He wanted me to be smart, to stand on my own, to be nobody's fool. He wanted me to know everything, live abundantly. He was proud of me and liked to show me off. In many ways he had great gusto for life . . . but all that worked against him in the end.

After church our family always got together at the big house, my grandparents' large two-story white frame house right in the middle of town, just two blocks from the bank. Before she left for church, Grandmother had put a ham in the oven and the cook would fry chicken, make dough for bread, and set it aside to rise so she could pop it into the oven the moment we returned.

Mother and my aunts would freshen up and then come down to set the table. I helped, carefully placing the old Haviland china and silver at ten or twelve places at the long damask-covered mahogany table. The kitchen was always the busiest room in the house. Grandmother would supervise, checking the yams, squash, mashed potatoes, English peas and gravy. There were always biscuits, gingerbread or cornbread, and pies or cakes. Sometimes she let me bake cookies or fudge, or my favorite, brown sugar nut cookies.

Granddaddy would head the table and ask us all to bow for the blessings, his soft voice praising the Lord and beseeching his blessing upon each of us at that long, beautiful table. He always ended, "Bless my darling," thanking God before us all for the woman who had blessed his married life. This became a symbol for me of everything good about Sunday.

Then he'd say, "Pass the yams and I'll carve this ham."

Sooner or later Granddaddy would launch into his favorite topics—hunting, fishing, banking or the history and politics of northwestern Georgia. I think I learned most of what I know about Georgia at his side. He told tales about the Cherokee Indians who had lived here long before settlers came up into the highland from Savannah. About our family dating back to the Civil War and before. About the growth of the railroads and industry in Georgia, and about cotton—the people who grew it, sold it, wove it into cloth.

Our Georgia was much different from the image that most people have of old plantation families. Plantation territory for the most part lies south of Atlanta in the great estates of the Fall Line Hills and on the wide coastal plain. Our family's roots go deepest in Gordon County which lies north of Atlanta just to the southwest of the Blue Ridge Mountains. Our way of life owes almost as much to Appalachia as it does to the style and customs of the deep South.

Granddaddy frequently pointed out that Calhoun, which sets high up in the Oostanaula River Valley, owed its growth to the Western and Atlantic Railroad, built in the mid 1800s, which linked Chattanooga in the north to Atlanta in the south.

It was this vital link that Sherman sought to cut on his campaign to Atlanta. He and the army of Tennessee, under General Johnston, fought skirmishes all through this area, culminating at the Battle of Kennesaw Mountain, not far south of Calhoun in June of '64. My mother's grandfather,

Captain Joseph McConnell, fought in Lee's Georgia regiment.

The women, of course, talked about baking and babies, the issues of home, family and town. Their talk was filled with the color and character of Calhoun. This approach to history back and forth across the Sunday dinner table forged for me a deep personal involvement with the life and times of my state and town.

Then Granddaddy would hold forth about banking or launch into some financial discussion. So I learned bits and pieces about the business world, the stock market, federal regulation and banking from the time I was a child. It was a rich, deep heritage, represented through the stories, loves, goals and aspirations of the people I loved best.

My granddaddy, Austin Banks David, of Dansville, Georgia came up to Calhoun as a young man after working in a bank in Adairsville, Georgia, ten miles south from Calhoun. He worked hard during those early years at the small Calhoun First National Bank, full of energy and lively optimism. He was the son of a farming family, but his dream was banking. He came into town around 1900 with a vision and helped make it into a reality. The bank was the cornerstone of the commercial life of the muddy-street north Georgia town that he loved. He put his life into it—he was the bank's greatest asset—and the bank helped and gave life to the community, transforming it over the years from a small rural hamlet to a growing town and center for the carpet industry.

Granddaddy was a portly man of medium height. He wore silk shirts with buttons on stiff collars, a black silk bow tie, silk socks and stetson hats—velour in winter and straw in summer. Banker's gray or blue suits with vests, gold cufflinks, a gold watch and chain, with a small gold knife on it, completed his usual business attire. An expensive cigar, often a gift from friends or family, was another trademark. He was very much a Southern Gentleman of the Old School.

He married Lilla Belle Barker, of Molena, Georgia, who diffidently did not claim to be "plantation wealth," though she might admit that she was Georgia gentry. She attended a girls' seminary school in Atlanta where the young ladies gave teas, studied the Bible, took instruction in painting and embroidery, lessons in dancing, practiced the piano and learned all the necessary "accomplishments and graces" requisite to being properly "finished." She was a large woman with fine features and long dark hair. She possessed infinite grace and charm.

I remember Grandmother as a gray-haired woman who was always the center of attention. I loved the smell of soft powder and perfume about her. She was a demanding but loving woman with a large circle of friends. She loved to play bridge. She had very bad arthritis in her knees and every summer during my childhood she went to Canada for treatments under the famous Dr. Locke. I remember those trips because she always brought home mementos of the Dionne quintuplets or pictures of Princess Elizabeth of England. She must have had fortitude and tolerance as well as grace and love to give up the pleasures and comforts of Atlanta and follow my grandfather and his dream into this pioneer section of north Georgia. They had three sons: Tom Banks David, William Bell David, and my father Claude Barker David.

My mother's people were also of a large old Georgia clan, the McConnells. There were McConnells stretched clear across Georgia from the Atlantic Ocean to Calhoun. Mother's ancestors were among the pioneers who settled Gordon County. Captain McConnell of the Army of Virginia married Julia Morris of Augusta. One of their sons, Hackett McConnell, was a prominent lumberman in Gordon County. He married Belle Shaw, my mother's beloved mother, about whom I heard so many endearing stories over the years. She died when my mother was thirteen and Mother moved from Calhoun to Atlanta to live with an older sister. But she was lonely. She remembered a boy in Calhoun. Ready to start a life of her own, she married him when she was 16 and he was a few years older. Mother was only 18 when I was born. I am the eldest of their three children; my brothers are Claude Barker David, called Barker, and Beverly Banks David, whom we called Banks.

I suppose that in some ways I was a pampered child. Maybe that is why I seemed to have been extra sensitive to both physical and more subtle forms of suffering. My earliest memory is of a commonplace accident, but it still stands out in stark reality in my mind. Even as I think of it now it makes me shiver.

I'm three and a half or four years old. I'm looking for Mother. I call her, and I hear her cry out. I run into the kitchen. She's standing there in the middle of the floor. Blood is running down her arms. She's holding both hands in front of her face, one hand grasping the other in a sort of contorted gesture of prayer. A butcher's knife is on the floor. "Get help, run!" she says.

"Daddy, Daddy," I scream. Where's Daddy—she's cut off her fingers, I think. The maid comes running.

She had cut her thumb to the bone, and the wound became badly infected so that she had trouble using her hand.

Why is that incident etched on my memory? It seemed to me, even then, to be some sign of the world's fragility and imperfection. It signaled some difference between the calm certitude of Jesus' encircling arm holding the children in the stained glass windows at church and the careless and un- predictable events of life.

Often as a child I was afraid to go to bed at night. I would lie awake crying or screaming with bad dreams, my stomach gripped by cramps. Mother would tell me it was only the shadows of trees waving on the walls, or the moon crossing through the clouds. But I dreamed I heard noises, voices, banging. Sometimes, too, I would wake up fearing that I heard someone coming up the stairs.

"Hush," Mother would say. "Nothing is going to hurt you."

"But I heard bad things," I'd cry.

"It's all right," she'd say, holding me close. "It's just the big trees outside scraping the roof."

And I'd shut my eyes, but demand that the hall light be turned on, and I'd keep listening for the longest time.

The days of my childhood were predominately happy,

however. Children, I think, are the ultimate conservatives. They thrive on routine and regularity. They love to have each day like the last (summer days if possible) surrounded by familiar faces. That was the great benefit of growing up in Calhoun in an era when families didn't move every other year because of job transfers. Now even Calhoun has become more industrialized and the mobility has increased. I learned early I could depend on people and trust them—I probably knew their parents, children, friends and neighbors as well.

"That's the key to country banking." Granddaddy was fond of saying. "I know a man's face and his character. I know his folks. I know he's got a farm and he isn't going to leave town. I know I can trust him and I know just how much I can loan him."

Granddaddy carried many farmers year after year due to crop failure, illness, farm prices. He helped hold farms and families together.

According to many stories and novels, the friendliness and familiarity among small town people can also create insularity and suspicion of outsiders. But what is less frequently reported of small town folk is the openness to and immense curiosity toward any newcomer to town. We children were especially fascinated by new students at school. It was this kind of curiosity that first drew Bert and me together.

Bert's father, Dr. Thomas Jackson Lance, was appointed superintendent of schools of Gordon County in 1941.

Dr. Lance already had a long and distinguished academic career. He started with a job as principal of a high school in Hopewell, Georgia. Later he taught English at Young Harris College and at Richmond Academy in Augusta. He was superintendent of public schools in Waynesboro, Georgia, from 1917 to 1930, and then was called back to Young Harris College to take over the presidency, a post he held from 1930 to 1941. Bert's mother was Annie Rose Erwin. She came from the same kind of devout Christian farm background, a family full of preachers, as Bert's father. She met "Jack" Lance when he was a teacher and she was a student at Young Harris.

As was usual for many community events, a reception was held for him and his family out on my granddaddy's farm. The "David Cabin" was the unofficial lodge hall, community center and church picnic grounds for Calhoun and much of Gordon County. The reception was a summer fish fry. Decorated tables were set up outside the spacious log cabin hung with deer heads displaying gigantic antlers. Seal and bearskin rugs from family hunting trips covered the floor. The gray-blue lake sparkled down a grass slope from The Cabin. A gentle and changing wind carried adult chatter and children's laughter across the wide expanse. It was a bright and sunny day, perfect for two blossoming sixth graders to get acquainted.

My friend Jackie and I were the "hostesses" for the younger group. It was our duty to see that Bert was introduced around. There is such easy and natural modeling in rural communities—children learn their roles, manners, and social graces right by their parents' sides. Young people called on elderly neighbors and relatives and there was a fine familiarity between them. We learned to take responsibility early and seriously—everything from household duties to entertaining—responsibilities that are not so easily taught in today's urban society with its greater drive and more distinct age segregation.

I think there must have been a little competition for Bert's attention between me and some of the other girls, because I remember finding some way of steering him away from the crowds around the table where the fried fish, rolls, salads, and hot dishes were being served. I escorted him away for the view.

"Would you like to see the farm; it's beautiful," I said.

"Sure, I guess so," he said shyly.

Then as now, I was the talker, he the listener. In this way we both had an opportunity to sound and measure each other's personality. And I was pleased that he was as tall as I, for by the sixth grade I had already reached my adult height of just over five foot five. (Bert's growth spurt was to come in high school when he grew a full foot taller than me.) Bert had a dark complexion, deep brown eyes. Very handsome, I thought. And he was comfortable with himself and me. And you cannot imagine how mature and accomplished he seemed to me because he had spent most of his life on a college campus.

Bert was born in Gaineville and raised in Young Harris, GA, a town as small as Calhoun. But Bert had spent all of his early childhood on the campus of Young Harris College, a small Methodist school in the Blue Ridge Mountains of northeastern Georgia. It was fascinating for me to meet a "college man," because Bert was used to a style of life much different from my own. There were faculty teas and student receptions and an exciting mix of intellectual conversation and theological discussion. He had been the "pet" of the college as the President's youngest son. He was also the first boy I knew who played tennis, which he had learned on the college courts. Calhoun did not have a municipal court or a pool, or any recreational facilities for that matter in those days. Bert made tennis sound very sophisticated. I was very impressed with him, too, because there was an oddly earnest, adult quality about him. He was more serious than the boys I knew, but he also was smart and clever, witty, in a way that most boys I knew weren't. He was verbal and quick. I mean, he could actually talk sensibly with a girl, or tell a real joke—whereas it seemed to me at that moment that most of the boys I had known all my life only teased and pulled pranks.

Naturally we talked about our families. Bert told me that his family had always been farmers, preachers or teachers. He said he thought he wanted to be a teacher like his dad or go to the Naval Academy and make a career at sea. He was one of those hill boys who dreamed big—and what was bigger than the sea. He also greatly admired his great-grandfather who had been a Methodist circuit rider in the Blue Ridge Mountains. The story was told that he was one of those truly heroic and largely unsung men who did more to open and secure the American frontier—from Virginia to

California—than all the trappers, cowboys and gunslingers combined. These preachers on horseback carried the lamp of enlightenment and the Word of God into some nearly god-forsaken hollows, mountains and plains. And Bert painted a vivid word picture of him.

Bert's great-grandfather was a forceful preacher and an uncompromising foe of those who preyed upon his flock. He fought to bring medical and economic relief to his poor parishioners and to stamp out the alcohol peddlers who were at the root of so much of their misery. The moonshiners warned him to keep away, to keep quiet, fearing that he would frighten off their customers and bring the law down on them. But he paid them no mind and persisted in helping and warning his parishioners. After one particular meeting up in the hills where he delivered a strong prohibitionist sermon, a gang of angry moonshiners ambushed and killed him.

It was this heritage of courage and service that Bert admired. And I admired him, hearing about it. I liked him. I felt sure that we would be friends. Maybe more. We walked around the lake and came back to The Cabin and the crowded tables where Jackie gave me a knowing smile.

From that very first meeting, I saw Bert almost every single day until I went away to college. In our small school we had almost every class together. We worked together, played together, held office in school clubs together, went to parties together, attended church and Methodist Youth Fellowship together. Now at age 46, I look back over almost an entire lifetime of standing by my man, and I am still filled with wonder at the continual unfolding of our relationship and love. Our sort of marriage was more usual in this country when small towns were the norm and even city neighborhoods were more stable, congenial, and homogeneous. Undoubtedly familiarity may, in some cases and in some marriages, breed contempt. But I believe that in most cases, at least in my own, it engenders love, continuity, respect and the sort of deep knowledge of one's spouse that cannot otherwise be matched. I believe real marriages are manufactured in heaven—but made to work on earth. Daily use is hard and wearing, so daily oiling with conscious care and consideration is necessary.

It is common nowadays for a married woman to know only one facet of her husband's personality—his domestic manner. His business side is virtually unknown to her. Similarly today's husband usually knows little of his wife's social personality. I feel I've grown as Bert has grown—spiritually, mentally, morally, and physically. In a town like Calhoun, business, church and social life intermingle, and husbands and wives are involved together in all aspects of community activity.

I feel especially fortunate because my life has blossomed with a family of its own with strong links across generations. I learned about banking on my granddaddy's lap and from my husband as he grew to become chairman of the same bank. While we've expanded our circle of friends, some of our dearest and oldest friends are still those from Calhoun. God has blessed us with such happiness that it would be wrong for us to reject him because of the burdens he asks us to bear. Everyone has to assume the trials of Job at some point in his life. And our family did have its trials and burdens. It is a family after all like every other, which means it is heir to all the misfortunes and mistakes that humans are heir to. But it is curious how we weave the fabric or our lives out of the crotchety characters, the trials and tragedies, the brutalities, weaknesses and enduring love that we find in families and community life.

In a small town the public school is one of the centers of community life and social activity. Mothers are involved in PTA, classroom projects and special events such as class plays, baking cakes, making costumes and so forth. In later years Bert coached Little League, was Cub Scout Master and refereed high school football games. Saturday afternoon football or Saturday evening basketball are events that bring out children, parents and grandparents and contribute to a small town's identity.

There is also a sort of false "Huck Finn" image about village school children; some people have the notion that most small town children would rather be out hunting or floating down a river than sitting in a classroom, but I, for one, always loved school. I liked organized activities; I loved doing things in groups; I loved formal occasions where I could dress up. I loved, in a word, being on stage. And school provided both place and occasion for all things I loved best. I can remember getting up on stage at the school, at age four, dressed in lace and organdy, to recite "Twinkle, Twinkle Little Star," and to practice my curtsy before the assembled hall full of mothers—all proud and powdered, dressed in their best and ready to applaud the performance of their neighbor's daughter. My Aunt Polly was my expression teacher. The art of elocution my grandmother had learned in girls' seminary was still flourishing in Calhoun in my childhood. So were the arts of warm sociability and tutoring within the family.

Because I learned to speak before friends, I've come to regard every audience as friendly. Today when I talk to groups large or small I always feel at ease. And it all comes from the discipline and practice I learned as a child.

Our elementary school was a red brick two-story building a block off Wall Street, the main street in town, right around the corner from where we lived. It was surrounded by a field of beaten earth that had been grass at one time, but which was utterly devastated by hundreds of running, jumping feet. There was a school bell in a belfry in the front of the building and we took turns ringing it by swinging on the rope. It must have been a substantial bell because its rocking swing would lift a child right off the floor. You'd pull with all your power and then, whoosh, up in the air you'd fly, laughing. A child who had been especially good or had done well in studies was allowed to pull the rope and ring the bell—so there was a sort of contest among some of us to see who would be selected most often. When Bert came to school a new competitor was added to the game.

I guess you might say I was a "persnickety" child. I liked things just so; I guess I liked things my way. Bert was always most solicitous and gentlemanly, even as a boy. How he first started calling on me was typical of his manner. Not long after the fish fry, he began coming to see my brother Barker, who was three years younger than we were. Bert would come by the house, knock on the door and ask Mother if Barker were around. Bert played the big brother part very well, but he usually steered the activities around to a board game, maybe Chinese checkers, Parcheesi or Monopoly, which three people could play. Bert was Barker's hero and I don't think he ever guessed the real reasons for Bert's frequent visits . . . but I did.

By the seventh grade we were sweethearts. And in English class that year the teacher intercepted a note passed between us declaring our mutual and undying love and pinned it up on the bulletin board for all to read. I was never so mortified!

Well, that's not quite true. For a proper and conscientious girl, I once trapped myself in a terrible predicament. It was in sixth grade math class, during the first big test of the year. We had these old, dog-eared, frayed, cloth-covered arithmetic books that for some unearthly reason had the answers printed in an appendix. The teacher had stapled the answer section together. No peeping—but what temptation! When one of the students discovered what test problems were being taken from the book, we copied the answers inconspicuously onto our work sheets. Almost everyone in the class was involved, except Bert, who, as the new student, was something of an unknown quality as far as our conspiracy was concerned. He had already established himself as the math whiz in the class. Someone had approached him, but he made it clear that it was against his convictions to cheat, and he turned the proposition down. Everybody raised their eyebrows at that. How could anyone turn down a sure thing. Amazing!

Came the fateful day. The teacher handed out the tests and three-fourths of the class was off and flying through the problems. Bright or slow, everyone was doing exceptionally fast and accurate work on this test because papers began to be returned to the teacher's desk in record time. But there was dear old Bert still plugging along, not half done with his problem sets. It was a little bit speculative about when to turn in my paper. I was finished so fast that I had nothing to do. I checked my circled answers twice, made sure I had copied the columns of figures correctly, judiciously decided to give one incorrect answer for credibility's sake, took a deep breath . . . and picked the wrong moment! I folded my work sheet with a neat vertical crease and rose from my desk to hand in the paper, when Miss Hill's growing suspicion finally came to the surface.

"Just a moment, LaBelle," she said. "Would you bring your book and work sheets up here with your test paper."

Panic! A quick examination of the back of my book revealed the awful truth. I had underscored the answers and written them in a column inside the book where the problem sets were. I had to stand by Miss Hill's desk to receive a reprimand before the entire class. The class was suitably squelched and trembling with a mixture of relief and trepidation. Each person was relieved that it was I and not he who was being pilloried, and each feared that at the next moment it might be he. Miss Hill promised a thorough review of the test papers, and the gloom darkened. The general antipathy deepened even more when at the end of the hour Bert handed in his test paper. There was some grumbling about "the goody goody bell ringer." I was sent home with a note to my mother. And an "F," Failure—the first of my school career—was recorded in the teacher's day book! The shame of it. Years before I had taken some pennies from my cousin's pocketbook and Mother had caught me. Scolded and spanked, I never did that again. But to be shamed in public was so much worse. How I cried. How embarrassing.

I vaguely recollect that Bert came over that evening to play Chinese checkers with Barker. I could hear their chatter through the shut and bolted door of my bedroom. I distinctly remember vowing to myself that I would never willingly unbar that door and show myself again to the callous and unfeeling world. Shame and guilt did teach me a lesson that stuck, however. It was better, far less painful in the long run, to do your own work, stand on the truth, and do what was right, than to go along with the crowd. I guess I found out that Christian virtue has practical value. I never cheated again.

Bert and I gradually became closer—after I finally un-barred my door (and my heart)—and I learned more about him and the influences on his life. One of the most signifi-cant forces came from an unseen hand—the effect of a death in his family a year before he was born. Bert, the fourth child in his family, was born long after Jack Jr., Bob, and Alice Rose. Jack Jr. was the apple of his parents' eyes. A strong, active, straightforward young man, he was active in many sports and physical activities, a picture of youth and health. But one evening in his room, after a scout meeting with friends, he contorted in pain, stumbled and fell. He had suffered a cerebral hemorrhage, and died within hours. Jack was sixteen at the time. This unforeseen, staggering loss had a profound effect on Bert's parents. Nothing is harder than the loss of a child. We grow closer to God's will as we age; we sense the blessing in the final touch, but the death of a young person seems to shake the very fibers of our faith. The Lances bowed to God's will. They grieved. They struggled to understand. They were lonely. They wanted another child. Bert was born a year or so after Jack Jr.'s death. The Lances felt that they had been given a second chance. Their new son was a special gift from God, precious to them and raised with special care and attention.

The lingering effect of the tragedy lay in the attitude of Bert's parents toward rearing him. They had a new, painfully sharp awareness of the fragility of life. Accidents, illness, the rough and tumble of a boy's growing up were viewed as potential menaces. It was not that they wanted to close him off from the world, an impossible task at any rate, but they kept closer watch and perhaps closer reins on Bert than they might have done if his brother had not died. He was the real baby of the family—12 to 14 years younger than his brother and sister. It was natural, therefore, for the whole family to spoil him a bit, baby him, give him an extra amount of "tender loving care." With this he imbibed all the drive, self-confidence and integrity of an only child.

Great things were expected of him, and in turn he ex-pected a lot of himself. Bert's father was also stern and upright in matters of morals and money. Responsibility, he felt, should be learned early and often, and Bert was expected to earn his own money from age eleven on. But his abilities were such that everything came easily to him—school work, leadership, even love for God.

Bert was one of those love-encircled children who go early, easily, wholeheartedly to God. He sensed that God had always been his friend, because his family told him that he was God's gift to them. Bert's journey with God was never a struggle. He was as faithful to his Lord as he was to his friends. His greatest talent perhaps was his natural appeal, his openness and ease at making friends and deep lasting relationships. He was so much at ease with himself, he made those around him comfortable with themselves. While I, like Jacob in the Old Testament, was still struggling with my angel, Bert had long since passed over the brook to openly greet his Lord and his fellow men.

As I said, by the seventh grade we were sweethearts—which meant that we walked to school together, ate lunch together, joined many of the same clubs and teams. We were a modest couple by today's standards. Only on occasional formal and public occasions, like school dances, did we even hold hands or demonstrate much overt affection.

On the whole my school days ran a smooth course, with an easy transition from Sunday school to public school and from school to summer vacation. In my early adolescence I went through an intense and deepening relationship with God. It's amazing how God prepares us for the different stages of our lives. At the point when we are beginning to discover ourselves, seek independence, and awaken to our nature as sexual beings, God seems to have built in a period of intense introspection and a kind of natural modesty. At the point where boys began to really interest me as boys, I became somewhat more reserved. I felt that I was experiencing feelings that no one else, especially a boy, could understand. I was moody more often, and my moods took wider swings. Some days were colored vividly by my moods—black days of depression, red angry days, green days of envy, and lovely pastel days of joy and happiness.

It was at this time, about age thirteen or fourteen, that I

came to a new understanding of my family and its problems. My father, it was obvious to me now, was a man with a drinking problem, and I began to recognize that it was not going to get better. I could remember the happy times, but I also remembered the times when drink made him angry and violent. It was obvious too that my mother was bravely bearing up under the strain, but that it was taking its toll on her happiness and her nerves, and our family life. Each day I wondered and dreaded what could happen. Mother tried to get Daddy to stop, and sometimes he would. He went away for treatments. Then he would make an extra effort to go to church, avoid his drinking companions, change his habits at parties. But the patterns of his life were set. He was a handsome, good-natured man, who liked people and liked good times. He was thought good looking. He had always moved among his fast crowd of boyhood companions who liked to party, liked to drink. He drank too much and alcohol had an immediate, profound effect. It darkened his moods and changed his behavior. Physically it was even worse on him; drink seemed to be actually destroying him. It made him sick. But still he couldn't stop for long. I would hear him come in late at night and I'd be afraid.

I loved Daddy and Mother and I took them constantly to God in prayer. I read my Bible daily. I struggled with the concepts of human habit and change. I prayed for a miracle. I made vows of self-sacrifice. I blamed myself. I found it hard to open up to my parents, and so I prayed all the more for God to help me.

Sometimes the days and nights were so bad, I even prayed for him to die. I prayed for God to cure him or kill him—just to bring peace to the family. And then I felt guilty! But I was learning something about prayer—that it holds you up even while you are questioning it; it is working for God's overall plan of good. It strengthens faith even if it does not immediately strengthen the body. God listened to my prayer which sought life and his will. I began to feel a closeness to God that I had not felt before, which issued in expressions of praise for his goodness, care and strength. I had to count on him. My serene family world was falling apart—where else could I turn?

My granddaddy must have sensed a lot about my feelings. He tried to be a second father to me. At four o'clock when the bank closed, he would frequently come around to our house to look in on us, and say, "Get a friend and let's go out to The Cabin." So I'd call Jackie, Betty, Bobbie or Sue Marie. He'd drive us and my mother and brothers out to the farm with him. There he'd often go fishing. He was a great fly fisherman, as was my daddy, who was an expert caster. They taught me, but I never had the patience it took to be an excellent fisherman. Or Granddaddy would talk with the tenant farmer and look into farm business, while we rode horses, played, read our homework assignments, or built outline rock houses on the slopes or played games like "Mother May I," "Fox and Hounds," and "Treasure Hunt." Granddaddy was always so generous and kind to me and all my friends. When I was a little older, he opened a checking account for me and advised me on how to use it wisely. Occasionally, my mother said, I used it to buy too many pairs of hose, but being active I seemed to have a run in them every day. Granddaddy's response to child or adult was always open and helpful. He believed in doing his duty, watching out for his neighbor, and he taught me by example.

"You look out for others, and the Lord will look after you," was his basic philosophy. One that I've tried to copy and live by.

Whenever he asked what I wanted for Christmas, I always made a long list! Then I'd ask him and he would say, "All I want is peace and kind words." And I'd laugh gleefully. It's taken a long time, growing up, but I think I've finally learned to understand what he meant—it was God's peace he wanted and the kind words and respect of his fellowman. That, it seems to me now, is a truly profound philosophy and the only truly desirable gifts, if they can be obtained. Granddaddy was given that reward. Like Solomon, he desired wisdom above riches, and in my little girl admiration I believed he was as wise as Solomon.

We spent so many golden days out at Granddaddy's farm. Of course we played hide-and-seek in the barn between bales of hay or tag across the fields. We went horse riding, fishing, and canoeing on the lake. At dusk the lake would become still, and the boys would walk out onto the dam and skip flat stones across the smooth, reflecting surface. On weekends, or in the summers, we girls would prepare picnic lunches or we'd roast hotdogs and marshmallows in the evening in the stone fireplace in the lodge.

I suppose I was given a lot of freedom, but it was not simple aimlessness. I was trusted, as were all my crowd, and since we did everything in groups, there was a sort of mutual chaperoning. Some young people got into trouble, but most of that was simple practical joking. I was prudish and didn't approve of stories that were told about my daddy, even the stories he told on himself, of skinny-dipping in the river in freezing January, and of Halloween pranks and other such careless rowdiness. I think my "persnickety" side disapproved. To me the proper manner of behavior was based on good sense, but more importantly I saw that formalities, manners and acceptable behavior must be based on a foundation of concern for one another that now I understand is the Christian standard for living together. The New Testament outlines the active love Christians must bear to one another—calling on the sick, comforting and sustaining widows and orphans. The life of the church resides in the formalities of care.

I know today that some consider "truth" to be a more important virtue than love. It is popular to say that when we are true to our feelings we are true to ourselves. To me this seems little more than willfulness. If I'm mad enough to kill, should I kill? If I'm angry and speak harsh and cruel words to someone I love—and I frequently do, unfortunately—have I achieved a higher level of virtue and personal truth than if I have kept still? I might think so at the time, but then why do I feel so guilty later? Why do I seem to suffer all the more when I have hurt someone I love? How does the "truth" of one emotional moment relate to my true feelings at future moments or to the "truth" of the designs and commitments and obligations I have made for my life, or to the truth of God's will for me? Love must transcend the moment.

I believe in being truthful to myself and others. But how can I be sure of the truth of my feelings? I try very hard to understand the difference between what I say and what I mean—but sometimes it's very difficult. Sometimes I unintentionally force away the very one I love and want close to me. I unconsciously erect walls that somehow I want them to scale or break through. With this sort of emotional confusion, who but God can keep me on track? He draws me back from my momentary needs and emotions to the good long-range goals, purposes and loves of my life. He does not want us crippled by the wild swings of desires, he wants us to go forward, true to the constant love that he implants in our hearts.

The manners, the "Yes, Sirs " and "No, Ma'ams" that my parents taught me were simply the social expressions of respect and Christian concern for another's feelings that helped keep me on track. They helped me to put others first, so that I would not fall into spoiled willfulness. The rules of decorum and behavior that were enforced in my life seem liberating in one sense—I did not have to create my own values and models. They were given, so I had more opportunity to select my role and to grow. So although we were given freedom we also were made to accept the responsibility for our actions. Our mothers taught us well, and then taught us to "Let your conscience be your guide." I, for one, did listen for the leading of that still small voice. Sometimes it was hard to hear—but the discipline of listening was good. It bred calmness.

Manners, discipline, duties and chores—those were our watchwords. Almost all the young people I knew had part-time jobs. Bert was as enterprising as a child as he was as an adult businessman—and he was as kind. He has given me many gifts over twenty-seven years of married life—some very expensive. But I'll never forget the first gift he gave me for Christmas the year I was twelve. He worked in the drugstore in Calhoun, part-time for ten cents an hour as a soda jerk. There he became acquainted with the fine and exotic cosmetics and finery desired by sophisticated women the world over, and he selected from this mysterious realm the most expensive and elegant deep blue gift box of "Evening in Paris" perfume and beauty set—$8.95. Eighty-nine and a half hours of work. Maybe it cost half that if he got it wholesale, and Bert always was a pretty good businessman. I was, of course, overwhelmed, thrilled. They were my first real cosmetics—lipstick, rouge, and that heavenly scent that I almost believed would transport me to Paris.

Bert had other jobs over the years—bagging groceries, bicycling special delivery letters around for the post office, and taking movie tickets. Sometimes we set up lemonade and soft drink stands for fun as well as profit, or sold shaved ice with sweet syrups poured over it and served in a cone-shaped paper cup. What a heavenly job! You may have called them something else—shaved ice or snow cones—but down there below the snow line in Calhoun, we called them snowballs.

The first taste tingled, saturating all your taste buds with freezing sweetness. Gradually the cold almost overcame the taste—your tongue and lips turned the color of the syrup, your finger tips got so cold you had to keep turning the cone around and changing hands. But your whole being was saturated with deliciousness. Only five cents.

The way we earned extra money was also characteristic of the way we lived and played—we created our own entertainment. I must have belonged to many, many clubs, church groups, teams, societies, auxiliaries and choirs in my life. We sang wherever we went. We played board games, card games, quiz games, circle games, team games. And though we frequently had adult supervision, most of our games and sports were of our own devising. There was no Little League; the boys played back-lot baseball. There were no soccer camps; we played kick-the-can in the school yard. Since Calhoun was small enough for all the adults to know all the children, there was no unsafe, off-limits neighborhood. We were allowed to roam or play anywhere, to create a separate and personal realm for ourselves outside adult rule. We were allowed to be children.

One of our favorite sports was sledding. It rarely snowed in Calhoun, and it never stayed on the ground, though we could go to see snow on Brasstown Bald, the highest peak in the state, sixty or so miles away. But we liked to go sledding on the heavy, flatbed sledges that were dragged behind mules when the farmers removed the stones from fields. The tenant farmer out at Granddaddy's place would hitch up a mule and children would pile on the sledge. Then we would "get-up" the mule, and holding the long leather reins we screamed and bounced and fell off and scrambled back up again, as our sled pitched and yawed over the ruts in the hard-packed road. What a great ride! I doubt if the children from Montana or Maine had any more fun gliding down a smooth white hillside than we did being jostled and jarred over the dry roadbeds of Granddaddy's farm. All this and warm weather too!

There was one job we did every year which was for us also something of a game—an enjoyable but serious activity. In the fall of the year, especially during early World War II when help was scarce, schools would let out for several weeks so students could help pick the cotton crop. For children who actually lived on farms it was an absolute necessity. The economic survival of their families depended on it. For those of us who lived in the towns it was a chance to help get in the crop and earn a little extra money.

I remember those soft fall days. Early in the morning we'd go out to the fields. There we would be issued a big heavy cotton bag by the tenant farmer or the field boss. The bag's broad strap would loop over my shoulder. Before starting, I'd look down the long rows of cotton and feel both anticipation and excitement. There was always a contest among us to see who could pick the most. Old or young, large or small, rich or poor, everybody was paid by the pound. It was a disgrace to have the lightest bag. And I'd vow to do as well as Bert and the boys.

We'd all start across the field in a staggered line that soon grew even more irregular as the fast pickers forged ahead of the slower. As we moved slowly forward and back across the field, we sang songs—school songs, MYF songs, picking

songs, popular songs we heard on "The Hit Parade" on
the radio. Soon the sun would be up. Though the days
weren't unbearably hot, I'd begin to feel the heat and the
increasing weight on my shoulder. The dust began to rise
and cover us. My fingers grew sore pulling cotton out of the
dry boll. There was an art to it that I never really learned. On
and on we'd go—taking frequent breaks to get a drink, or for
most any other excuse. Sometimes I'd straighten up for a
minute and gaze around the field and listen to the song of
the meadowlark. It was different for me and the others for
whom picking was not a living. To us it was a game, we were
like the meadowlarks skipping and singing over the field.
We didn't have to come back tomorrow if our shoulders were
too sore.

All of us would take a long lunch break and we'd spread
our picnic baskets out in a shady spot. It felt so good to lean
back on the partially filled cotton sacks, under trees at the
edge of the field. After stooping along for hours, even the
ground felt soft and welcome.

Our cook usually made sandwiches and lemonade and
cookies and fried chicken. Food never tasted better. The
mere cessation of movement felt pleasurable. And in the
quiet and rest you could almost hear some spirit moving
over the brown, dusty fields. And nature showed forth all its
beauty. I sensed a continuity with those who worked the
earth, stretching back even to the biblical Ruth who labored
in the "alien corn," gleaning the dry fields.

After lunch my resolve to bring in the biggest bag wa-
vered, but we'd all go back and try to work until dusk. I was
fascinated by the minute-by-minute transformation of the
day: the moving clouds, changing wind, variations in color
and light, the sounds of insects, the gradual tiring of the
songs we sang. I've always watched the clouds, reading
stories and finding images in their change and passage. My
load became heavier and heavier. My shoulder felt as if
somehow it was dragging behind me. And the soreness
worked its way down, finally settling in the small of my
back. My throat was dry. This was the time of day when the
shadows lengthen and my thoughts turned naturally in-

ward. I thought of Millet's famous painting "The Angelus," of the simple farmer and his wife bowing for evening prayers in the field, a copy of which Mother had at home.

Finally the day was over. The light was dying. The field was quiet. We lugged our sacks in to be weighed. Two big men, tenant farmers, would take it from us and sling it high up on a scale held aloft by two others and weigh it in. Mine were never very heavy. Not enough picking—40 lbs., 10¢ a pound. And the paymaster counted out the money then and there. And though I never came in first, I rarely came in last, and the pride of actually getting through the day was almost as satisfying as the money. I went home tired but happy. I knew that I didn't have to come back tomorrow unless I wanted to. I was thankful for the financial security of my family. The sunset seemed to restore my soul and a good night's sleep restored my body.

This work gave me tremendous insight into the plight of those who work year in and year out on such backbreaking, manual jobs. All across the South there are those whose lives are tied to toil. Picking cotton, harvesting soybeans, digging peanuts, working in carpet factories and weaving mills. While picking cotton I learned about the dignity of labor and also the toll it extracts from laborers. It taught me not to be afraid of hard work, and it taught me to appreciate commercial goods, soft and lovely clothes, appliances, luxury items—everything that is produced by the sweat of someone's brow. Because of this, I've always believed that goods should be treated with respect, not wasted, not tossed aside because of a change in fashion. I like things that are simple, but elegant. I like beautiful, but sturdy, serviceable furniture (with four big sons that really was a wise choice), and good classic clothes and durable goods, because someone's pride and labor produced them.

These years of transition from late childhood to early adolescence were colored and overcast by one long pervading fact and mood—the war. It was on everyone's mind constantly: some angle, response, or image about the war seemed to occur in every conversation. Every family had a son or father or sweetheart overseas or in training or in the hospital. We read the newspapers and were glued to the radio nightly to hear Gabriel Heater, H.V. Kaltenborn, Edward R. Murrow and others deliver the news from the warfronts.

We were the home front. We did our share. Picking cotton. Saving aluminum foil, paper, string, scraps of metal and rubber. Waving to the soldiers going through town on maneuvers. We endured the shortages gladly. Gas rationing and food stamps became a way of life. Mother adapted recipes using less sugar. I barely noticed what was missing—it was a simple reality and necessity. There was nothing I would not have sacrificed if it would have helped our cause. Every night I prayed for peace and for all those suffering. I sometimes struggled with the absurdity of war, and begged God to intervene and to stop the Axis armies. It was difficult for me to understand why God tolerated this human folly that was hurting millions. At Sunday services and mid-week prayer groups we brought our pleas to God. Everyone pulled together to help the mother of a soldier killed in action. Mother worked at the Red Cross, rolling bandages, knitting sweaters. We sent victory blankets overseas and packed what are now called "Care packages." Sometimes we'd include hand-knitted scarves. It sounds ridiculous, but here in this cloth and carpet center I learned to knit squares for afghans on a pair of long steel nails, because of the "needle shortage."

Bert and I and all our friends—we were the children of the War. We had a special sense of being set apart from those who were just a few years older than we. We were old enough to understand the horror of the times but were too young to serve. Too young to count, but old enough to be affected by war's horrors. We felt deficient in a sense, born too late to help. But we also felt spared by God, held aside to be another generation. We were indulged. Adults looked at us in a way that was full of protection, as if they wanted to hide us from the present, keep us children. To become a man or a woman was to face war and death.

Sharing everything, we children grew up in the Looking

Glass world of war. And so we went through all the motions and emotions of normal school years. But the attention of our teachers, our pastors, our parents sometimes seemed to shift, veer off like that of a person who hears a sound far in the distance. Then they would come back to us and concentrate on us with renewed solicitude, as if they wanted to screen us in part from the nightmares of the world. And all the time we played at growing up, holding hands, taking tests, playing sports and games. I was one who believed in not growing up too quickly. I was convinced I should not be kissed until I was sixteen. (I didn't quite make it! But it was worth waiting for.) We ran home to listen to the radio and check the newspaper for descriptions of assaults and battles and victories.

Prayer was fuel for our spirits. It was as much a part of every day as breakfast, lunch and dinner. Everyone had a loved one in the service somewhere. You'd see people pick up a newspaper, scan the headlines, and grow still. They were saying a spontaneous silent prayer. Much later Bert and I took a trip to Europe and I saw barbed wire separating countries for the first time. It evoked memories of the war years.

With the world at war, my own family troubles were put in perspective. It was hard at home with Daddy still drinking, but he at least provided us with financial support. He was too old and had too many children to be drafted. We were so much more fortunate than the millions who were homeless or enslaved, or in the midst of fire and bombings and bloodshed. I think I began to see that God works on every scale of his creation, caring about the smallest movement in one person's heart as well as the vast cataclysm of armies clashing across continents.

Those things which I could not understand were made acceptable by Jesus' firm assurance. I trusted that God held the whole world in his hands, as he did my own insignificant life. I knew how he had given me comfort when there had been trouble in our own home. I trusted him to bring comfort to those who were suffering the havoc of war and to ultimately bring peace to the world—even over the obstinacy and perversity of man. He after all was the Comforter. He was the Peacemaker.

To a degree, we children also glamorized war as well as feared it. We saw it on the silver screen. War was John Wayne and "The Flying Tigers," Humphrey Bogart in "Casablanca" and James Cagney toppling Japanese battalions with his bare fists. It was one way we could make sense of the sacrifice, but sometimes the cruel reality pierced through the facades of protection thrown around us, and our illusions came tumbling down like the walls of Jericho.

In 1943 Bert's brother Bob went down in the Atlantic on the U.S.S. Buck. He had been an officer in the Navy. He left a young wife and a three-week-old baby boy. Bert and I were in the seventh grade. We had just recently declared our affection for one another. How could such adolescent affection, which expressed itself in teasing and games, express itself in a moment of death and loss?

I remember sitting in Bert's parents' parlor. The big old clock on the mantle sounded like a heartbeat. Everything seemed close, unreal. The pastor was there. Bert, his sister, his parents, other friends and family, neighbors. The room was hot and crowded and I felt trapped. Some people were crying. Bert was red-eyed, ashen-faced, but stoic, dressed in his Sunday black suit. People paid their respects to his parents and stayed to eat cake and coffee from a buffet table, talking quietly.

I was caught in a conflict between emotion and convention, between giving and restraint, between love and fear. We had never been open with our affection. We were just two children experiencing puppy love. Quietly I went over to Bert, burning with anxiety least he reject my gesture of concern, or some adult see me and look askance. I simply stood by him and took his hand. We stood together, not looking at each other, facing a roomful of mourners in silence like two frightened children facing the reality of war.

Gradually the high tension of those war years escalated the problems in my own family. For years I guess I had seen it coming, but I had repressed it. As a child one tends to see the world simply as it is; a child doesn't understand how a family's life can be other than it is. You accept your family as you find it. All mothers are the way your mother is; your father is as others are. So, though I had a growing realization of my father's problem with alcohol and the wearing it caused on my parents' marriage, I was still not fully prepared for the separation into which mother was finally forced. I was fifteen. There were arguments. There were fears and violence. And finally Mother made an arrangement with some friends. Together they would purchase the Rooker Hotel in downtown Calhoun. She was to manage it. When all was settled, and the help was hired, an apartment was set up for my brothers, Mother and me—a freshly painted apartment-on the first floor near the back street. It was private and I often used the back entrance. We ate in the hotel dining room—and I had snack privileges in the kitchen. That part was wonderful.

I tried to think of this change as an adventure. I had always liked the hotel with its high ceilings and big, dark rooms lined with damask draperies, the hardwood halls, and marble-tiled public rooms. The dining room was where the junior and senior classes always held their dances and proms, and I saw myself giving private parties like these. Mother did let me have parties sometimes after evening meal hours, when the hotel was quieter. I was Cinderella at the ball. Rapunzel in her tower. It was sad to be away from our house, but it was also a relief. A relief to be free from the fights and the fear. I was outwardly calm and brave, but my composure might have fallen if not for Bert and Granddaddy and Mother and God.

I discovered something during this time. I discovered that *I* needed God's help. All my life I had been praying for the hurts of others. Oh, I prayed for myself as all children do constantly—for toys and gifts and dreams and all the things that matter very little. And God had heard and always been kind. Now I was beginning to learn what Granddaddy's "peace and kind words" meant. I had never had such a need, never been hurt at such a fundamental level as to feel broken, to feel torn apart, to feel damaged so that I needed God to heal the devastation within. But I needed him then.

"Yea, though I walk through the valley of the shadow...," Psalm 23 says. And the Shepherd was with me.

On the surface, everything was the same. The pace of my day-to-day life didn't miss a beat. I had moved only a few blocks from where I used to live. And yet in some ways everything was different. I arose at the same time every morning as I had before. But time seemed altered. I had the same memories. But my own history seemed to be given a new interpretation. I saw events in a different light. I had the same friends, the same family all around me. But I may have sometimes felt a bit uncomfortable and uncertain. How did others see me? How was I to act when I was with them? Who was trustworthy? Who could I talk to? Who would love me?

Granddaddy was my rock, my link with the past, my bond with my daddy. By this time my father was very ill and spent most of the time in hospitals away from home. In a town as small as Calhoun there are few secrets about marital changes of this magnitude and so all my friends knew. The separation was accepted, no big deal was made of it. Bert and my friends stood by me and helped me. And I got myself through classes and clubs and activities. Mother and I were really close. She did not abuse Daddy or try to turn me against him. She tried, on the contrary, to find ways to assure me that he loved me and that I should love him. She told me she still loved him, that at some level there was an unchangeable, irrevocable bond of love and memory, but that she simply had to live in the now and at the practical day-to-day level of life. And at that level their marriage had failed; the pain was no longer tolerable. She had to leave for her children as well as herself—and we all had to agree, even though our hearts were sore. But acceptance developed slowly through the years. It was no quick rending, but a day-to-day growth of sadness and separation.

It was only in subsequent years that I came to fully appreciate Mother's courage. Separation or divorce is no easy matter. Raising three children alone is not a light job. Managing a hotel is no vacation. Doing all this in the same small town where you had lived as the wife of a prominent businessman could have been humiliating. But Mother didn't give up on her friends. Nor did they give her up. She went to the same clubs and bridge groups and to the same church where the love of God and the acceptance of Christ had always been shown her. And she refused to give up on Daddy. The separation was her last resort—her final attempt to try to bring him to his senses—to test whether this radical separation could help him break the hold that alcohol had on him.

When I think of sinfulness, I think of bad habits. It is as if we are in thrall to some unwillable force inside us, to Satan, and it is only by dependence on God that we can overcome him. We can do nothing by ourselves. "I do not do the thing I want," says Paul. That's true. Why? I've thought about my own bad habits. I have a hasty and sometimes horrible temper. I know that. Why can't I keep my teeth clenched when I feel anger welling up inside me? I know people who can't stop eating. They look at the scales. Make vows. Go on crash diets, emergency exercise binges. They want with all their will to lose weight and then they go back to sneaking cakes and candy and junk snacks. Why? Why did my daddy drink? Why do I want things that aren't good for me? Why do I run from God when I'm on top and crawl after him when I'm on the bottom? It's the grip of humanity. The mark of our insufficiency. The flaw of fallen beings. But when we realize that, then we must cry out, "O wretched me—forgive me God, cleanse me and claim me—I claim you through your Son who died to save me from my sins and imperfections." And then God opens our eyes and we are reborn in his Spirit.

Daddy struggled, but he was sick. Physically sick. He had cirrhosis of the liver. When we moved out he was still working, but he was at home part-time, and in and out of the hospital. He grew sicker. Finally he was too sick to drink, but then it was too late. He made his peace with God at a terrible cost. Two years after the separation, when I was seventeen, he died.

I prayed for him every day during his last illness and I

prayed even more after his death. I wanted to pray him into heaven. I promised God I'd go to church every day of my life and pray for him. But I knew at the same time I wouldn't and so I feared that my failure would jeopardize his salvation. God knows the fears, vows and anguish of a bereaved adolescent, but I did not. I was filled with grief and the impotence of doubt. Mother saw my condition and tried to comfort me. One day I broke down crying and she took me in her arms. We were in the bedroom of our apartment, and I remember the yellow gray afternoon light filling the room like a soft cloud.

"It's over now. You don't have to grieve, LaBelle," Mother said.

"I'm not grieving. But ... Daddy's life seems ... unfinished. I ... did he have a chance to make his peace with God, Mother?"

"We have to leave that to God. But I'll tell you this—your father was a good man. He had his problems. He had flaws as each of us has in some way. But he never consciously hurt anyone. Not consciously. You don't have to worry about him. God knows what he was like. God forgives."

I felt a thrill. I believed she gave me a word directly from God. It eased my doubt and relieved my guilt and grief. Through her, God released my mind from worry. An adolescent cannot do some things for herself. I was not capable of working out the logic of this situation as an adult could. I needed what, in fact, I received—a sign from God that acted as a pardon, a reprieve, a release from the irreconcilable emotions and problems that tormented me. And I was able to praise God and turn my father over to him in assurance of his forgiveness and his perfect will.

He was gone—gradually the emotions, the sorrow, the guilt, the loneliness passed. This too passed. Life went on. My mother rebuilt her life and I continued with mine with all the supportive friends that had been with me since childhood. We joined clubs. We took comfort and pleasure in groups. Bert played football; I was a cheerleader. Bert was President of Beta Club; I was secretary. Bert was editor of the high school newspaper; I was Society Editor. Bert was senior class president, I was secretary-treasurer. We were both on the debate team and in class plays.

I especially enjoyed working on the paper which, though it was only a few sheets of mimeographed paper, contained our own words and was put together by our own efforts. We celebrated team victories, printed outrageous gossip under veiled identities or initials (not hard to guess who was who out of a class of thirty!), editorialized about the leading issues of the day, such as cleaning one's locker, new uniforms for the basketball team, and the dangers of smoking in the restrooms. How many hours did we struggle to get the stencil cut and run off just right? Why did it always seem to come out crooked? Bert had to draw the masthead by hand each issue—two fighting yellow jackets, which was the name of our football team and the name of the paper.

I can still smell the pungent ink that was poured into the rotating drum of the mimeograph machine. I remember the way the stencil always wrinkled and how the thumb and forefinger of my hands turned black, despite my effort to be careful. In despair I often called in some cooperative, less fastidious boy and let him put the stencil on straight. Bert was my favorite assistant! Production was neither the Society Editor's forte nor her favorite task.

We also had homework. Homework which we delayed, did in groups, rewrote from encyclopedias, struggled with, hated, handed in with pride—or despair. On the whole I didn't dislike homework. I studied long and hard. It was something all good school girls were supposed to enjoy. I worked. I worked at the pink dressing table in my bedroom, at a meticulously clean but unproductive desk . . . or lying down on my bed, sofa, floor . . . sitting at the kitchen table. Always a book. Always the lights burning with a weak yellow glow. Many times I worked until midnight. I was assiduous: I was going to ring that bell! I wanted to perform well, do the proper thing, please my mother, do my very best. I felt that doing any less was only cheating myself.

I might not have known it then, but I truly believe now that as Christians we are called to do our best. Discipline is one extremely important key to victorious Christian living. We are to learn to overcome all the impulses that lead us to indulge ourselves and not think and work for Christ. The Christian road is a hard one, but it is the most rewarding road.

I truly believed that hard work would take me anywhere that fit into the will of God. I had a dream. I wanted to be an actress on Broadway or in the movies. See Hollywood and the Pacific Ocean. I wanted to go North to school. See snow. I've always loved its white, quiet beauty. See the Empire State Building and Times Square. I believed that doing my homework was the first step to accomplishing my dreams. I had drive. I competed with Bert as only boy and girl friend can. And when we graduated, I was valedictorian and he was salutatorian. Staying up all those midnight hours until the work was done as well as I could have done it had paid off.

Years later I became familiar with Jimmy Carter and his book *Why Not the Best*. I recognized that his philosophy was the same as mine. He probably learned it in homes and classrooms in Plains similar to those in Calhoun.

In our small town schools there was tremendous optimism. One had to expect a brighter future; without this hope there was little else to inspire us, at least by today's standards. We had old school books, no computerized study programs, no TV instruction, no modular formats, no multitude of electives ranging from woodland survival techniques to filmmaking. We had Readin, Ritin, and Rithmetic. We had teachers who believed in progress, who believed our generation should receive a good education. They believed in their students, and believed that God's hand should be a guiding force in teaching and learning. With that we lacked for nothing. Our school day began with prayer. I still believe in that. What our children miss without prayer is incalculable. We said the Pledge of Allegiance and prayed for the President, the generals and our men. It would have been considered unpatriotic not to be optimistic. We had to believe we would win the world for freedom and for the justice of God. Our job as students on the home front was to do the very best we could. Our education was guided by moral and biblical principles. Learning was not merely an option, not only self-serving—what we learned was to be used for the benefit of man and the glory of God. Why not the best, indeed? It was an absolute necessity.

The senior year of high school was one of the most poignant years of my life. I had the conviction that I had reached the crown of creation—was at the height of my powers and sensitivity—and yet there was a suspicion that I was really innocent, not truly tested. I looked around at all that was familiar and seemed to see it for the first time—knowing that soon it would be for the "last time," when I went away to college.

I spent hours looking through college catalogues and dreaming. Mother advised me that Agnes Scott in Atlanta was a good school, but I wanted to go North. I applied to Vassar and Wellesley and many other schools. I wanted to act. Bert and I were in the senior class play together. I could imagine nothing better than acting. I thought a career in the theatre would be a life-long senior play. Mother said that Agnes Scott would provide excellent preparation for theatre. I sent out applications in the spring of my junior year and acceptances started coming back from many schools by the fall of my senior year. I was ready for a big break. I was going to assert my independence.

Bert was going to Emory. Mother quickly pointed out that Emory was only a few miles from Agnes Scott. Agnes Scott was also close to Calhoun, so I would be able to come home whenever I wanted. I didn't seriously consider it, but I did apply there rather late. A letter of acceptance was returned.

Mother took me to Rich's Department Store in Atlanta to shop for graduation and to begin to plan my college wardrobe. We picked out light pastel summer dresses, bobby sox, a couple of sweaters for college, and for the senior prom the most beautiful white off-the-shoulder ball dress I had ever seen. It was trimmed in gold thread and sequins. We went to the huge book department where I bought a collegiate dictionary, a thick one-volume encyclopedia, a new Emily Post, and a couple of good novels. I grew up with Emily Post. Mother believed in her for every social occasion from writing invitations to setting the table. Emily Post was the ultimate word. Now I think that strict attention to form can be foolish—good manners are really based on thoughtfulness and courtesy.

Mother also managed to steer me over to the Agnes Scott campus. It was a lovely place—not far from Emory, not too far from Calhoun. I was a Southern girl, after all. I loved the South. I was beginning to consider Agnes Scott as a possibility.

"You'll like Agnes Scott," Mother assured me a few days later, as I returned the student entrance forms.

"I'm sure I will," I said.

She was happy. I was her only daughter. She was still so young, only 18 years older than I. We almost could have been sisters. And from an early age we had come to rely on one another. We comforted one another and cried together when there was trouble at home. We prayed together for strength. And since holidays could be especially lonely for her, I took it upon myself to see that they were happily observed. I worked to make Christmas special. And now that Daddy was gone, I tried to make it especially gay and festive. I decorated the tree, always making sure that there was a special present for her underneath. I maintained a militant cheerfulness for the holidays. We were essential to one another, so naturally Mother wanted me close by, and Agnes Scott was ideal in every way.

Atlanta

Atlanta is the largest city of the deep South. It was born in 1833 as a railroad junction, and was first called Terminus, but then the tracks pushed onward west and north until it was no longer a terminus but a junction, a mighty crossroads, and it needed a new name to fit its growing image. It was totally destroyed in 1864, but it was reborn out of the ashes of the Civil War. Out of the devastating fire that millions saw represented in the movie, "Gone With The Wind," the city sprang to energetic new life.

Atlanta has always been a city on the move, growing, building new tracks, stringing out telegraph wires, and launching airplane routes in all directions. Bert tells an old joke that illustrates the fact that Atlanta is the transportation capital of the South. Two old friends die the same day and meet in the lobby of the Celestial Transportation Company. "Which way you going, up or down?" asks one old friend. "Don't know yet," says the other, "But it's a sure thing I'll be changing trains in Atlanta." That story is as true today in the jet age as it was in the era of iron rails. Delta Airlines, the major passenger and freight carrier of the South, has its home in Atlanta. And all the railroad tracks and truck routes up and down, east and west still meet here. Fifteen hundred manufacturing companies call Atlanta home—automobiles, airplanes, chemicals, furniture, steel, paper, fertilizers, soft drinks, processed food are made here. It is also the financial center of the Southeast and home of the Federal Reserve district bank.

But Atlanta has a deep personal meaning to me as well. It

is the place where I went as a child to go shopping, to the theatre, to the museum. It represented to me the larger world. Bert and I lived our young adult lives in its orbit. Our professional lives have moved like a pendulum, swinging to and from Atlanta. Atlanta has been the chief stage for the dramas of our adult lives. It represents for us another aspect of life in Georgia. It is another place to call home, another place to seek opportunities to do God's will.

As the summer after high school wore on, I looked forward to going to Agnes Scott as if it were an invitation to a dance, or a command performance. I was ready to throw off some old habits and old acquaintances in order to experience new ones. Bert was one old acquaintance I secretly thought I might be leaving behind. Oh, he was good, he was kind . . . but he was familiar. I was glad he would be nearby in case I needed him sometime, or in case I were stuck on campus some Saturday night without a date. But there was a whole city full of boys I hadn't yet met—young executives-to-be from Georgia Tech and Emory.

Agnes Scott is in Decatur, a suburb just east of Atlanta. The campus is beautiful, built around a quadrangle, replete with rolling lawns, huge old trees, distinguished red brick buildings. It was home away from home for about five hundred young women. It was a new experience for me to be in an all-girl institution. There was a surprising, but subtle shift of emphasis. I think the competition was keener than in high school—the more aggressive you were, the better your grades. And of course there was that typical bravado of college youth daring things that were not considered proper at home. Thankfully our escapades were not too dangerous in those days. The rules at school were very strict: no smoking, no drinking, appropriate dress required, campus curfew at 10 P.M.

Naturally I had to break a few of the rules or I would have felt I was not living my life on that "broader stage." Though I had never smoked before and had no real interest in it, I was determined to try it. Everyone was doing it, and if some student officer or housemother should chance to happen by a place where there was smoking, suddenly the windows would fly open and girls would be fanning the air with books, towels, anything they could lay their hands on to drive the smoke out of their tobacco dens. I thought it extremely sophisticated and went through the ritual of initi-- ation with my roommate late one evening, after a long "philosophic" discussion had convinced me that some of my inhibitions needed to be unbridled. We slipped out to an off-campus drugstore to experiment.

"Don't shake the match, and don't light the middle of the cigarette. What's the matter, are you nervous?" my room- mate asked.

"Don't be childish, of course I'm not nervous."

"Inhale then," she counseled.

I did and my mouth filled up with acrid hot smoke and my cheeks bulged out.

"Don't gum it to death. You're breathing like a fish. Breathe it into your lungs."

At first I didn't seem to remember how to take air into my lungs, but when I finally did, a blast furnace explosion went off in my chest and a tornado of soot, ash and molten lava swirled round and round and mounted to my head. I felt my face flush and the pit of my stomach grow cold. I began to cough uncontrollably.

"That's it," said my roommate. "Now you're smoking."

I hated it at first, but what else could I do? Admit it and suffer the derisive abuse of all my friends, the most sophisti- cated girls on campus? I kept at it religiously, rising from a few strategically puffed cigarettes in social situations to per- sonal orgies of a couple of packs a day. After a while I didn't even have a headache and I felt so sapient, so intense in creating a cloud of industry above my off-campus study nooks. Again I was plagued by the "math-book syndrome." Hundreds of girls smoked thousands of hours and all went without detection, but I was caught every other time I picked up a cigarette. The first time a couple of student government officers caught me at the drugstore. I was even campused a couple of times. You can't imagine what those lonely date- less weekends did to my self-esteem.

Smoking is one thing I didn't pray about, I guess because it was such a consciously chosen vice. It's hard to commit to God what one has objectively decided. That would be admitting that he might know better than I. I guess I felt in my heart that it was a bad habit leading to bad health, and bad manners. But I disregarded all this for the camaraderie of the girls and later out of habit. I smoked for six years.

Then one night I woke up from a dream in a cold sweat, convinced I would die in six months if I kept smoking. Convicted! I saw a terrible scene—a growing cough, the visit to the doctor who sadly shook his head, the funeral—it was horrible! My career as a smoker ended right there. My small internal voice had become a ringing death knell. I realized I was doing something I really didn't want to do in my heart of hearts. And I've learned that's a good sign of sin.

It's amusing to think of this juvenile "depravity" now. And it's sad to think how the risks of conformity have risen for the generation since I attended college. The Surgeon General has proven that cigarettes are deadly, but today's social passwords are marijuana and hard drugs. They are a far more devastating menace to young people.

So many of our habits seem painless or harmless enough. But Christians must understand that all behavior is a form of faith in action. Ideally man's mind is to be focused continually on God in prayer and praise. In I Thessalonians 5:17, Paul tells us to "Pray without ceasing." Action that is habitual has become unconscious, and our bad habits make us inattentive to God and to his rule over our bodies and lives. Our bad habits are a retreat into forgetfulness, self-deception or sometimes even a kind of listless death wish. The person who overeats, drinks or smokes is a person unconsciously seeking oblivion. And oblivion is in the direction opposite from God who calls us to himself to be believers with both mind and heart. We all are sinners—great or small—but God forgives and wants us to try to better ourselves each day.

I did not devise or realize this argument at the time I broke with smoking. It evolved slowly over the years, as I confronted one form of self-deception, one bad habit after another. And as I watched my own children grow up.

Agnes Scott was a good place to learn, even with all its restrictions and heavy academic pressures. It gave me something to react to. It set behavioral and intellectual standards. I was really redefining my character in those early days at school. I went to English literature classes a wide-eyed romantic, and found hard analytical work was expected. I discovered the terrible shock that most freshmen experience—the shock that your classmates are at least your intellectual equals, if not your superiors. Coming as valedictorian of a small class of thirty, I had expected to sail right through college as I had high school. I was used to the grind, but not the competition, and when that first hit me I stumbled. In some classes I did well, but in others not so well. And I discovered that I liked boys and parties and extracurricular activities—which was really no surprise. So, much of my energy went into social pursuits.

One course that I did take seriously was a year-long course in Bible. Everyone was required to take it at this Presbyterian school. Daily chapel was also required. I knew the Bible, I thought. I'd read it and had it read to me all my life. This course should be easy, I thought. Wrong! We wrestled with one problem after another. How could a loving God order the killing of innocent women and children? How can the hatred and vindictiveness in some of the Psalms be justified? Could Jonah really have lived inside a big fish for three days? Linguistics, history, archeology—and that was just the beginning. About the second week of the class I began to see the Bible as a deep mine. You could work on the surface or the first level and discover the truth of God's Word for your life, but you could also dig deeper and deeper and continue to find new meaning for your life and never exhaust its infinite resources.

Bert and I occasionally went to church together, either at Emory or in a nearby Methodist church, but most of the time we spent Sundays with our families back in Calhoun. When we attended churches in the Atlanta area, we missed the familiarity, friends and fondness we felt at our hometown church.

I found during this first year at college that I still liked Bert, but that I could also take him or leave him. We had been as close as a brother and sister for years, and I think we both wanted a small respite and a chance to see others and the world on our own. When I heard he was dating a particular girl, I did not begrudge him—though I might have let it be known that there was someone whose fancy I had caught. After those first few weeks, when we saw each other because we longed for someone familiar, we drifted apart, together and apart again naturally, easily and with no ill feelings on either side.

Bert was busy anyway, going through the ordeal of getting into a fraternity—the hazing and house duties and all. And I was being rushed around to parties and all sorts of other social affairs, so there was little pain accompanying our romantic break. Bert finally pledged at Sigma Chi and was initiated toward the end of his freshman year. We were both too busy with new things and people to worry about old ties. We didn't miss one another very much. This period gave me a chance to see Bert more objectively.

Bert was a happy person, a pleasant, sincere young man. He trusted people. He wasn't always looking for hidden motives, nor did he always look for angles. He was generous. He always seemed to have a gift or a bouquet for me on every special college day or holiday. He had a good sense of humor (though I'd heard most of his jokes). He was easygoing, yet he had goals. He was ambitious, but not in an aggressive, pushy way. In high school he had been voted most likely to succeed. He wanted to do the best he could. His early training and his early ambition led him toward a service-oriented career. He thought he wanted to teach.

I liked what I saw. I was less sure about what kind of person he saw in me. Taking after my name, I was always something of a "belle." I could be flighty, but I hoped he saw the inner me which was serious about the purpose of life. He had always said I was pretty, but I always felt that beauty was in the eyes of the beholder—I had only been fortunate to be among those who looked on me fondly. I had been chosen Miss Gordon County the summer just before college, but I didn't put much store in that. My self-esteem was healthy, but I had an even healthier sense of modesty which sometimes made me shy. Sometimes my tongue was like the wicked kind Proverbs and the New Testament book of James complain of, and I had used it on Bert from time to time.

I suppose I had my good points, too. I enjoyed people, and could put them at their ease. I knew how to listen. I had a strong sense of myself as a Christian, and I was growing toward understanding that the serious purpose of life was to serve the Lord wherever I found myself. I hoped I had the kinds of organizational talents that make a good wife and mother . . . but I wasn't looking that far ahead just then.

How quickly things can change. In the spring of my freshman year a group of my classmates and advisers and boys from a Georgia Tech fraternity went on a weekend trip to a lodge up in the Blue Ridge Mountains at Lake Rabum. We were all in a gay party mood. It was a cool, lambent, late May day. The pines were fragrant and the spring flowers in bloom. Outwardly I was enjoying a beautiful day, but privately I had been feeling ill and the pain made me increasingly more and more uncomfortable.

In the evening we all went to the lodge for dinner and a song fest in the large hall around a huge fire in a natural stone fireplace. At first I thought I was simply sitting too close to the fire, but when I moved away from it and still felt as if I were burning up, I started to worry. Then I came down with severe cramps. The pain was worse than anything I had ever felt. "Food poisoning," they said. "Try to vomit." But I had eaten little, and no one else was ill. "Where's the pain?" they asked. And I pointed to my right side and then I heard the whispers: "Appendix."

Finally they called the doctor. He examined me and said, "Get her to a hospital; they'll have to operate."

The cramps and nausea swept over me like huge breakers of the ocean. I seemed to go down, almost lose consciousness, suffocate with pain, come up gasping for air. I prayed. I was so afraid. I couldn't believe this was happening. Like most young people I had felt "immortal." Death was something that happened to old people, or to someone else. I had been rudely awakened by my daddy's death. It had awakened me to the fear of the fragile nature of existence. But now my life seemed to hang by a thread and I couldn't believe it. I saw myself as someone in a movie—the heroine is ill, rush her to the doctor; she'll be all right in the second act. But would she? "Poor girl," they'd say, "she died of a ruptured appendix. She was so young." I held on with the fierce tenacity of fear and faith. "I want to live," I prayed. "I have so much yet to do."

They wrapped me in a blanket, and helped me out to the car. I stretched out on the back seat, while a friend drove. We were miles from nowhere, high up on a mountain. The nearest hospital to Calhoun and home was in Dalton, seventy miles away. I'll never forget that ride. It went on and on in a long gray expanse of time—falling down the mountain, down and down. Every turn in the road seemed to shift the pain from one side of my body to the other. I never lost consciousness, but I was nearly delirious. Everything appeared so strange and I couldn't separate thoughts in my head from what was going on around me.

Someone had called my mother, and she and Granddaddy were waiting at home to take me to the hospital. They rushed me into surgery and I remember the bright, bright circular lamp with three rings of coronas that suddenly went fuzzy when someone clamped a rubber mask over my mouth and nose.

I woke up feeling cold spears of pain sticking my ribs, stomach, back. "Dear God, where am I?" I prayed. My eyes were open but I couldn't see. I was a newborn kitten. I began to cry for Mother and Granddaddy. "Let them come in," a voice said. And then I felt two hands take mine and another hand laid on my brow.

"You're looking well, Missy," Granddaddy's voice said.

My lips were dry and cold, and seemed non-functional. I knew what I wanted to say, but couldn't say it.

"Don't try to talk," Mother said, as she patted my hand.

"You're going to be all right, Baby. You just had an appendectomy."

"Missy, praise God you're all right now. We're going out so you can get some rest. Do you understand?" Granddaddy said.

I barely nodded. I didn't want them to leave. Their touch seemed to be my only contact with reality. Granddaddy placed his soft, warm hand on my forehead. I heard talk, other voices. Feet shuffling. They had left. But his hand seemed still to be pressed in prayer on my forehead. I could feel it, the tender imprint of each finger—the warm contact with the realm of the living. It stayed with me until I drifted off the iceberg of deadly cold pain into a warm, forgetful sleep.

It must have been touch and go. Another hour or so in the car and I wouldn't have made it, they said. And my convalescence was long and slow. Mother came every day. In those days they kept you in a hospital bed too long. Now they get you up and moving, so all your systems start functioning again. But I was flat on my back for ten days. And then I suffered through a long recuperation at home that lasted the whole summer. I missed final exams at Agnes Scott.

One of the first get-well cards I got was from Bert. He sent camellias, my favorite flower. He was tied up with finals, but promised to come and see me as soon as school was over. He did. In fact, after he returned to Calhoun for the summer to work as a part-time teacher at one of the county schools, he came every day to see me.

The first time he saw me, he looked as if he'd seen a ghost. I don't think I ever saw anyone so shocked. And I burst out laughing—which hurt all over. I guess I was pretty wan and wraith-like. I had lost weight because I couldn't eat. Immediately he pretended nothing was amiss. He brought a rose for me to place in my hair. I've always loved to wear flowers in my hair, and used to pin formal corsages behind my ear. Bert told me about finals and teased me saying that my "hospital gambit" was the sorriest excuse for getting out of exams he had ever heard. It was surprising how much we had to talk about.

Bert came day after day, and at first I put it down to his usual tact and kindness. Then I thought, well, maybe he wants to go steady again. But finally I understood something had changed. We were no longer children. It was that simple. I had nearly died, and he had nearly experienced an ultimate loss. I could see he did not want to risk such a loss again. Bert was serious. The boy who had grown up by my side, who teased me, went hayriding and swimming with me, the boy I thought I had left behind when I went out into the big world was telling me in soft and not yet verbal ways that he wanted me by his side for the rest of our lives. And I wanted that too.

I did get better. The summer dragged on and I made arrangements to finish my courses and catch up on my work. I saw Bert often. He was enjoying teaching, and he talked about what a different experience it was to be on the other side of the desk. He clearly liked working with young people. He thought he had found his career. When I went home he made "house calls." He was the best doctor for my spirits, keeping me up on local news, gossip, what he was reading, how he felt about teaching, what his plans were for the coming year.

Mother had moved from the hotel to our old house in Calhoun and our front porch became the gathering place for all our old high school crowd. The times they were there were good, but it was a long summer. Almost everyone has a period of "dead time" in their lives. That summer of recuperation was one for me. What did I really want to do with my life? Was acting a real option? Did I want a career, or marriage? What had this close encounter with death shown me? I suspected that it showed me that what I loved best, wanted most and could do best lay close at hand. I could search the world, only to find the best place was in my own backyard. I loved my family, Calhoun and I guess I admitted (tentatively) that I loved Bert. I wanted to spend my life with them, to help them, to share my love with them, which Paul teaches is the goal of a Christian community. Yet all these things were whirling like a cloud in my mind. I was waiting for the fulfillment of my will, when in fact I was really waiting for God to accomplish his. God's will.

In the fall we both went back to Atlanta, but we kept in touch by phone and Bert would come by for study dates. We kept borrowing cars to go see each other. We'd go to the library for awhile, but then we'd usually escape early to a place where we could listen to music or just quietly talk and have cokes. If the day were nice we'd sit out on the grass or under the arbors on the campus grounds. The round of these days was slow and lovely. And I think that we were more concerned with each other than with studies. We finally acknowledged that we were, in fact, in love. To me it revealed something important—love makes all things new. We who knew each other so well, for so long seemed to be seeing each other for the first time, discovering so much we never knew about the other and ourselves. In the late fall of that sophomore year Bert gave me his Sigma Chi fraternity pin.

It happened one night while we were sitting out under the arbor near my school dorm; we both came to the conclusion that we ought to get married and finish school together. We were very "academic" about our decision and the positive educational values which would accrue from marriage. Bert wanted to tie the knot right away, but I was the kind of girl who wanted to get married only once in her lifetime, and I wanted to do it right. I wanted a traditional wedding, lots of parties beforehand and a big church service and reception. We publically announced our engagement in December and set the wedding date for the following September.

We decided we'd both transfer to the co-ed University of Georgia at Athens. Bert was happy with a September wedding after he thought about it awhile. It gave him a whole summer to work and save money. I took some University of Georgia extension courses to make up for credits I was going to lose in the transfer and for an English course I had failed thanks to my cross-town romance with Bert.

I had been "married" once before—in a "Tom Thumb" wedding at age five. It was a kind of dress up, play-acting that taught stage presence. In reality it was a mock wedding ceremony that was something little girls and their mothers especially enjoyed. (I'm not sure about the little boys.) It was a special honor to be chosen the bride. But it did signify the importance that marriage had for young girls. Our whole growing lives were directed toward marriage and assuming our roles as wives and mothers. All the girls I grew up with had marriage as their primary goal and concern. I remember that when I was a teenager our congregation was building a new church and there was a general meeting to discuss how the new church should be built—what things we wanted changed. My suggestion was characteristic of the romantic ideals we girls cherished. I suggested that the aisles of the new church be made wider to better accommodate a bride, her father and her wide dress. Some of the adults may have been amused, but we were very serious about such things and the pastor and the building committee and *their wives* did see the logic of my suggestion.

Bert and I scheduled marriage counseling with our pastor. And of course we got a lot of unsolicited advice as well. It was a learning experience. Most people made us really think. They impressed on us the seriousness and the long-term commitment marriage involves. I forget who used the analogy of a man going into the army—he worries whether or not he is really making the right choice and will be able to stick it out for four years. "But in marriage," this person said, "you're signing up for a lifetime hitch." Another person told us, "You both know how hard it is sometimes to live with your mother, father, brothers and sisters—well that's what marriage is like. And if you live your three score and ten you will spend more time with your spouse than you have with your parents or than you will with your children. Are you prepared to see the same face across the breakfast table for the next forty or fifty years?" I think Bert and I sneaked a nervous look at one another. It was a sobering thought.

Our pastor emphasized that marriage was the making of a covenant. The covenant was binding for life, but it had to be renewed every day. The pastor also underscored that a married couple is the basic unit of worship. "A family is the smallest church. You should pray together daily," he said. "And learn to forgive. Make the effort to be the first to say, 'I'm sorry.' Be the last to take credit."

Now Granddaddy was to lead me down that widened aisle. A marriage in a small town is an important event. Everyone is involved. For months preceding it there are bridal showers, receptions, luncheons and dinners. The bride-to-be collects a trousseau, silver, china. The community takes an active part in setting the young couple up in their new home. And then everyone turns out for the wedding.

I wore a white satin and french lace bridal gown with a cathedral train. The lace panel down the front of the princess-style gown was set off by long, pointed sleeves with satin-covered buttons at the wrists. My veil was a long, full silk illusion, appliqued with lace inserts and seed pearls. I carried a fan encrusted with small french sequins and beads with gardenias, which Bert had given me as a gift, attached. The bridesmaids wore long pale green satin dresses and carried lace fans I had given them. And the groom's attendants wore white ties and tails.

We were married on September 9, 1950, two weeks before school opened. We were both 19. It was a real big production for our small town. There were eight groomsmen, eight ushers, all good friends of Bert's, and eight bridesmaids, plus a junior bridesmaid and one junior groomsman, and one little boy who was the ringbearer. I was the second bride to be married in our new church, which was just across the street from Mother's new house. Granddaddy was proud and characteristically straight and erect. But there were tears in his eyes as the bridesmaids walked down the aisle.

"We love you, LaBelle; we love Bert. But old folks always cry when they see the young ones starting off on their own." I hugged him and, pulling aside my veil, kissed his soft old cheek. The Wedding March began and we started down the aisle. When he answered the preacher's question, "Who gives this woman to be married...," he returned my kiss before releasing my hand and turning to go.

The reception was a success. We had a caterer come up

from Atlanta to Calhoun and everything went just as my mother and I had anticipated. During the summer, while we had been planning the wedding, Bert was planning our first home. He rented an apartment in Athens, near the University of Georgia. The landlord agreed to paint it while we were on our honeymoon on St. Simon's Island.

We were already packed. And after the wedding and reception at home, we piled into a new 1950 Chevrolet coupe which my family had given us as present and headed to St. Simon's Island. Bert's uncle was the night clerk at The King and Prince Hotel, and with dutiful young-married frugality Bert had arranged with him for a special rate. Like most newlyweds we were self-conscious and shy, and we spent five lovely days alone by the sea on the caramel-colored sands, walking around the marshes and down the back roads. It was the beginning of a life-long love affair for me—with Bert and with this beautiful piece of Georgia, the Golden Islands.

It ended all too soon—school started in another week—and we found ourselves packing once again. Bert had pre-registered as a junior at the University of Georgia in business. I enrolled there in elementary education. But I was primarily concerned with setting up our first apartment. It was a pleasant place of three rooms on the first floor in a large old private home just three blocks from campus. Other students lived there along with Mrs. Allgood, the owner. She was like a mother to us all, helping me put up curtains and clueing me in on all the secrets of cooking—at which I was none too professional. I spent hours on the phone getting recipes from Mother, but even then Bert suffered through frankfurters in barbeque sauce on numerous occasions. Blessings often come in disguise. This was the origin of Bert's interest in cooking, and over the years he became something of a gourmet cook, omelettes and desserts being two of his specialties.

It was a tranquil year with few demands other than papers and finals—which then seemed traumatic enough. Though our parents feared we'd never get any studying done, we both did better academically than before we were

married. No time wasted on cross-town dating as before—
now we were together. Bert's study habits, especially, improved. He was taking his courses more seriously now that
he was a married man. Mine improved too. I returned to the
honor roll as in high school.

But I remember that first year primarily as a year of talk.
How earnest we were! Entertaining, studying, or dreaming!
Young couples just starting life together. How many eve-
nings did we spend visiting other young couples like ourselves. We sat in small parlors with parent-borrowed,
piecemeal collections of furniture arranged with loving care.
We ate; we gossiped about teachers and classes; we settled
the world's problems including the Cold War. We argued and
debated foreign affairs with great untested idealism. We
walked and talked. And I remember leaving so many "discussion parties" late at night to return to our own apartment,
where I'd lie down with tenderness next to my very special
husband—mine—feeling that all the danger in the world had
passed away. The world was ours.

Bert worked the following summer, between our junior
and senior year, at the Calhoun Bank, learning the business
under my granddaddy's tutelage. He also liked doing part-
time work with children. Almost every day he'd take a group
of boys to play tennis or some other sport. We saved a little
and supplemented the rent and tuition money that our
parents contributed to our education. We didn't have much
more than enough for groceries and a few incidentals, but
that seemed so abundantly much. We were rich—as rich
then as we ever were to become.

Then in our senior year I became pregnant. We were both
so happy. But how was I going to continue school? Bert was
worried about money. We talked it over and over.

"Our parents can lend us some to help with the doctor
bills," I said.

"They've been too generous already. I don't want to be a
burden," he said. "I'll quit school for a year, we'll save a little,
and I'll finish up later."

I wasn't so sure. But then Granddaddy offered Bert a
full-time job in the bank. We could have the baby back home

in Calhoun, with family all around, so I agreed. It would be wonderful, just as everything had been wonderful. Danger and uncertainty had passed from our young world.

So we came back early to Calhoun, as we suspected we eventually would, to start our lives in a new place. We rented the second floor apartment in an old home on North Street and began to fill it with furniture collected from both our parents and with a few new things. We added slowly, piece by piece. Bert was eager to get started at the bank. He never did anything half-heartedly; he used all his energy and was always optimistic.

Bert started as a teller, learning the profession from the ground up, and very soon he discovered that he really liked it. He had a natural knack for one of the essentials of banking—making friends and meeting people openly and honestly. Many people think of banking as a "stuffy" profession, and banks as sort of Victorian Temples of Commerce—cold marble halls of strict formality. They also talk about "bankers' hours" as if they were late starters and earlier finishers—that's not so. Bankers work long before and after they open their doors to customers. Banks also live as other businesses do, by attracting new clients—both borrowers and depositors. It was in this area that Bert had an obvious talent. He was always positive and helpful. He shared himself, his time and his advice with the farmers, small businessmen and homeowners in and around Calhoun, and they liked and trusted him.

I busied myself setting up our household. I was happy. Everything was going perfectly, just the way I'd planned. Bert was continuing to go to school and Mother was helping me set up the apartment. And then I began to have difficulty carrying the baby.

Fearfully, I went back to our physician. He examined me thoroughly. Nothing seemed to be wrong. He took blood samples; then he asked Bert in for a blood test. When the results came back from the lab he called us in. I remember waiting in his office—with that empty doctor's office feeling. The numbing wait, the worry, the inability to talk openly. The dull and ominous mood which you fear will never go away settles over you. The doctor asked Bert and me into his inner office and we sat down wide-eyed, holding our breath. He laid out all the facts as directly and as plainly as possible.

"You probably won't be able to carry full term, and your chances of having other children are not good," he said.

We felt the earth sinking beneath us, leaving us stranded in mid-air. We quietly asked, almost begged him to give us some hope, but we knew that the best hope rested with another, higher Physician. Dr. Norton gently explained the problem. He and his wife had had the same condition.

The baby, he said, probably had a blood problem. I had RH negative blood; Bert, RH positive. If the baby had RH positive blood like Bert's, my body would react to the child's blood as it would to a foreign substance and produce antibodies to counteract it. The antibodies could attack the baby's red blood cells and destroy them. The situation made carrying the baby difficult, but the greater danger came after birth. The child would become anemic and jaundiced. If the destruction of the child's red blood cells had proceeded too far it could lead to retardation, cerebral palsy, or both. To protect against this the infant would have to undergo a complete transfusion right after it was born. In those days the operation was dangerous and critical.

Nowadays there are modern medical methods to treat the problem right after conception and while the baby is still in the uterus. But in the early 50s such methods were not known—the transfusion after birth was the only way to save the child. And that meant that there could be great problems during the pregnancy. And I was already experiencing difficulty. I had to spend almost all of the last six months of my pregnancy in bed at home and sometimes in the hospital. It was a trying and frightening time.

Bert and I wanted children so much. We looked upon them as God's gifts. And now we were told that this baby might not survive and that the very fact that I was carrying this child was causing the creation of antibodies, which would make having other children even more difficult and dangerous.

Bert was very concerned for me. He saw me lying in bed

day after day, and I think he thought of the time he almost
lost me. He was sad that the joy we most longed for, the fruit
of our love and marriage, might be impossible. My mood was
sometimes sad, but he sat by my bedside every evening in an
old borrowed easy chair and did work that he'd brought
home from the bank.

"You know I want this baby, Darling, as much as you
do," he said one night. "But I don't want you to take any
chances. I ... I want you too. . . ."

"You'll have me. Remember what the pastor said, you're
going to be looking at me across the breakfast table for fifty
years." He bent and kissed my forehead, and went back to
his work—always glancing over his papers at me for some
sign of trouble—as if he could detect some secret, external
sign that would become visible on my face.

What a good man I have, I thought. The pastor was
right. Marriage is more than love. It's ... it's a church that we
spend a lifetime building, day by day like one of those
Medieval cathedrals. Master builders, stone masons, gla-
ziers, sculptors, wood carvers spent a lifetime of work, joy
and sadness to build up such a lovely structure.

I spent so many nights crying. I remember lying in bed in
that upstairs room and gazing at the shadows that passed
across the ceiling like ghosts whenever a car went by outside. I could feel my baby inside, kicking, growing, alive.
And I'd be overcome with feelings of fear and guilt, worrying
that my own body was revolting and attacking the child I
loved and wanted as much as I wanted life itself. When I felt
him flutter inside me I thought of a butterfly: small, fragile,
tucked away in his cocoon growing into a creature of light
and beauty. Only he was much more than that—a human
child, made in the image of God. I held to the hope that the
secret chemistry of life, which God ordains and controls,
was working against the dark chemistry of death. God's
hand was on me. I knew it was. I was afraid, but I trusted
him. I had doubts, but I had a foundation of hope.

God teaches us acceptance. What can we do? We can
trust in God or throw ourselves into darkness. We can't
change the fate that befalls us or wave a wand and be

transported to a better world. We can only say to God, "Yes, your will be done," or plunge into impotent rage, cowering fear, or inhuman indifference. Whether we are in a hovel in India, or a mansion in Manhattan we can say yes to God and life and strive, or say no and die. I put myself in God's hands and said, "I want this child with all my heart, I will endure anything for it. I am not afraid of pain or danger. But as your Son said in Gethsemane, 'thy will be done, not mine.' *Thy will.*"

It was hard, but eventually after fear and trembling and pain, I did have the baby. He came three weeks early. The doctor had to induce labor in order to protect against further blood damage. And when he came he was little, his blood count was bad and his life was held by a thread. We named him Thomas Bertram Lance, Jr., and called him "Tram."

What joy and fear we felt. We had him, could hold him in our arms, comfort him, feed him, love him—but would we be able to keep him? This was an even greater test. To have lost him, not knowing him, was one thing. To know and love him, and then lose him would be so much worse. Day after day we watched and prayed. We took one day at a time, the same way we built our marriage. The way you build a life—or save one. . . . We nurtured him and prayed for him for nine more months while he was under a cloud. Colic, weakness, pneumonia, nine hospital stays. And then he came out from the shadows and began to grow and eat and kick and scream like a healthy baby—he began to fly like a butterfly. It was as if he were born a second time to a strong and vital life.

When people ask me how we could endure Washington and Bert's hearing before the Senate and his resignation, when they ask, "How could you stand it?" I say, "Easily." That was only our job, not our life.

"What has hurt or touched you most?" they ask.

"We're just like you," I answer. "The human things, the family things hurt most—just as they give the most pride and joy. We've lost loved ones, borne and raised children, seen friends divorced, felt illness, watched death—if we haven't learned to live and trust God after all that, we wouldn't be human as God wants us to be, trusting and dependent on him. We wouldn't be Christian, we wouldn't have learned anything from life. Washington was not a major crisis in our lives," I say.

Bearing children and raising them, I was to learn, is no easier than building a marriage. *Labor* is such a good word for birthing and rearing. And yet each one of our boys is a precious gift. All the more so because it looked at first as if we would not be able to have any. But we wanted more, and through prayer we decided to try again. And miraculously they came with far less trouble and less Rh problems. They arrived each with his own personality, demands, skills and talents. Tram, our first, came in 1952. Then David in 1954, Stuart in 1960, and Beverly in 1961.

I ruptured a disc in my back during my labor with Stuart. And after he was born I spent months flat on my back in traction. We rented a hospital bed and set it up in our house, so I could be close to the family. It was one of those periods where I was again taught patience. I took up painting, embroidery and knitting, making things for Bert and the boys. I monogrammed every shirt, pair of pajamas, and robe of Bert's and the boys. I read a lot, especially the Bible. The Psalms were a great help to me.

Only those people who have had a back problem or some such injury know how terrible constant pain is. It grinds you down until, like Job, you cry out for justification. The Psalms is the book for those who suffer—because cries of praise echo the cries of pain. I read somewhere that conflict and suffering are at the core of our human nature. If being human means that we must suffer, we have only two choices—to suffer and seek God, or suffer and refuse him. It's terribly ironic and sad that so many people choose the latter. It's lamentable that others take so long to give up to him the very burdens that weigh them down in despair.

When I was in traction I could have thought of myself as someone being tortured on a rack. Instead, I tried to see myself as a student of patience. Patience is one thing I've had to learn the hard way. I've always been a go-getter—impatient for work, for fun . . . go, go, go. How do you learn to slow down? I wouldn't recommend it as a conscious choice, but believe me, with your head flat on the bed and your legs propped up in the air with weights hanging from them, you are definitely slowed down.

I had severe back problems for four years. For four years I had unremitting pain. At the time you think you can't stand it. It is both a comfort and a temptation to cry to God for a healing miracle. He wants to hear our pleas and our needs. He has promised to answer prayer. But our demands for healing are based on human timing and reasoning. God will answer—but in his time and for his reasons.

It is a mercy that when relief comes, pain is not held in memory. It passes. I was supposed to have an operation, but by the end of the fourth year the trouble subsided on its own. My body was healed. Did I learn patience? Not completely, certainly not constantly. Sometimes I was so frustrated and hurting I'd throw down my embroidery and gaze up at the ceiling through a red rage of impotence. But in the long run I did learn something. That pain has its limits—in severity and duration. It passes. All things pass. God and time can heal. Having felt this pain I knew there was nothing worse physically to fear. God's time and God's reasons must be foremost, and I struggled to understand his purpose in my pain. Job was tempted to doubt the Lord. He did not. If pain teaches us to trust, we have learned a great, great lesson. A lesson worthy of its cost. It is through suffering and even by martyrdom that faith shows itself to be more firm than the forces of this world. By example of courage and forebearance we can best witness to others about God's gifts of love and salvation.

Those early years of marriage were "children years." We moved from the apartment to a small rented house right off Wall Street. Then in 1956, as the family grew, the house grew. We added rooms. We added dogs. We added up the bills. At first Bert was working at some part-time jobs—refereeing football and coaching baseball and various other evening jobs. But he gradually became more and more involved in bank work, and he rose from teller to managerial positions.

Bert made the most of his time at home with the boys. We were usually able to have all our meals together. The boys got out of school for lunch and Bert would also walk home, so we spent noontime together, which most families miss. It gave us a mid-day pause for prayer and sharing the day's activities around the table. Our sons were fortunate to have a father like Bert. He is calm. He is reasonable and slow to anger. I am not always so slow. He was a man they could bring their problems to, and they could expect sympathetic advice and a firm, disciplined follow-through. But at the same time he helped them set high goals.

I had to admit, too, Bert was a good husband. He didn't look like the sentimental type—not in his conservative pin-stripe banker suits. But he was. He is. He never forgot to bring home a present of camellias or candy on Valentine's Day, and little remembrances throughout the year. In fact, Valentine's Day has always been a special day for us. And we celebrated by a night out—alone—for a change, and Bert might have a sentimental jeweled pin or charm for me.

During the period that I was raising my family, Mother remarried. She wed Ronald Chance, a Calhoun lawyer and they had one son, Ronald Jr.

Children years are years of gentle chaos. Not the kind where the house topples down—but the kind where one shoe is always missing, someone is always sick or unhappy, there is a different club meeting for a different child every afternoon and evening. There is yelling, crying, fussing. Yet, in recollection, even the horrible seems to fade into a pleasant memory—a gentle flowing stream of life, widening as it flows.

Each child was so distinct. Each had a variety of special needs and interests. For one collecting was a passion and the house filled up with model airplanes, stuffed birds, coins, etc., etc. For another hunting and fishing were ruling passions. One wanted to drive a tractor and work on a farm. One took paramedic training, working for an ambulance service.

Each of our boys taught us something—about life and about love.

There were an infinite number of near misses, illnesses, accidents. But the one I remember most vividly involved a kind of miracle. One day when Stuart was just a toddler, we had a visit from the Orkin man, the exterminator. Because we were having a problem with field rats, he laid down poison in certain places around the house. One place, for some unknown reason, was under the cabinet on which the television sat. Bert's mother was visiting that day, and she just happened to see the baby put something in his mouth.

"Heavens, what's he eating?" she cried out, and ran over to catch him.

"He's got a fistful of rat poison," I screamed. She knocked his hand away and forced whatever she could out of his mouth with her finger.

I ran to get a washcloth and we cleansed his mouth as well as we could. I didn't know whether to get him to drink water, milk or something else—or try to make him vomit. Mrs. Lance was sure she got everything out. Stuart had stopped crying from the scare we had given him, and he seemed fine. I called our doctor but he was out, and since there was no change in Stuart, the crisis seemed to subside. By the time Bert came home late, the baby was in bed and I even forgot to mention the incident.

But in the middle of the night, I woke up in a terrible fright. I dreamed the baby was dying. I woke Bert up out of a sound sleep and we went to check Stuart. He was sleeping soundly. I told Bert about the poison and I was so distraught I urged him to call the doctor.

"It's 1:30 in the morning," he said.

"I can't help it. Something's wrong. I just know it." I picked up Stuart and he didn't seem to stir. He wasn't very responsive. "Something is wrong," I said. I began to get panicky again.

Bert called and finally aroused Dr. Purcell, our family physician. He asked what kind of poison Stuart had eaten, and how much. We gave him the brand name. He said he'd check with the poison center. In a while he called back saying that they couldn't exactly determine the ingredients. Finally, at 4:00 in the morning, the doctor found the name of a representative of the Orkin Company, and got him out of bed. The rat poison contained an ingredient which caused internal bleeding. We rushed Stuart to the new Calhoun hospital a few miles away. The doctors examined him carefully and gave him vitamin K shots. If we had waited until morning it might have been too late.

I'm sure that God spoke to me in that dream. I might have had any kind of worried dream. But I dreamed of a child dying. That dream saved Stuart's life. Maybe when we sleep our attention can be more readily gained by God who calls to us constantly. Certainly I've awakened from sleep to write poems that seem to be inspired by God. Dreams, I believe, are part of our experience we too frequently ignore. They help us get in contact with ourselves at a deeper, subconscious level and occasionally they may be a medium for God to give us a message we need. The Bible tells many stories about how God speaks to people through dreams and visions.

When David was five or six years old a simple tonsil operation nearly cost him his life. I was worried about him and decided to spend the night in the hospital after the operation, although the doctor assured me there would be no danger. There was even another child David's age there to keep him company. The next morning the other youngster was up early, feeling fine and eager to go home. But David was just lying still, breathing hard. I knew there must be something wrong, and I summoned the intern. He examined David quickly and put in an emergency call for help. One doctor came running out of an operating room where surgery was in progress. They rushed in an oxygen tent and a whole team of doctors and nurses started working on him. Apparently during the night David had contracted pneumonia. He was sinking away when the Lord tapped me on the shoulder and led me to act.

The list of children's tantrums, temptations and tragedies is almost too long to recall. Once Beverly and Stuart fell into a yellowjacket's nest up in the woods on a hill above our house where the boys had a hideout or play hut. Both were stung. Stuart pulled his younger brother out of the hole into which he had fallen. Beverly was badly stung on the face and was swelling so rapidly he was hardly recognizable. I called Bert and then rushed Beverly to the car. It wouldn't start. Frantic, I started walking toward town, carrying the numb child in my arms and praying that we would make it. He was having more and more difficulty breathing and had become semi-conscious. God answered my prayers. Bert met me on the road, he picked us up, and drove us quickly to the hospital. Beverly was stung in over five hundred places. The stings were so bad that for three days in the hospital they didn't know if he would live or die. His face was so badly swollen it looked like he was covered by a stocking. Again the Lord was with us, and he survived.

Getting a message through to me—from God or anyone else—was no mean trick while the boys were growing. They each had Cub Scouts, clubs and so many activities, and Bert and I had the same. *Preoccupied* was a sign that hung permanently on the door of my mind. When Bert ran for governor years later, a sketch was written about me for news releases. It listed the following activities (which made me sigh, "No wonder I never got around to doing anything in those years—I was too busy!"):

"LaBelle is active in the First United Methodist Church, having served as a Sunday school teacher of children and adults, as president of the local and district United Church Woman and also as an officer of the North Georgia Conference for two years. A charter member of the Calhoun Jr. Women's Club, LaBelle later became president and in 1958 was honored with the Walter R. Thomas Citizenship Award given by the State Federation of Women's Clubs. In 1958 she was selected Seventh District Homemaker of the Year, being honored at the south-eastern Fair in Atlanta. [Sounds like I was rarely at home—making anything.]

"In addition to these activities she qualified as an

instructor and for several years worked in the Red Cross swimming program. [How I loved those bright days in the water with eager, splashing children— though sometimes I almost became waterlogged!] Also, she was a volunteer Gray Lady at Gordon County Hospital for over three years.

"LaBelle has been involved with Cub Scouts, serving as den mother for over six years. She also was actively involved in the PTA and is a past president of Calhoun Elementary PTA. Through these school years she served as grade mother, program chairman, and social chairman. Needless to say, she knows how to make pies, cookies and punch. [Needless to say!]

"Mrs. Lance (LaBelle) feels that civic duties are very important and has served on boards of the Community Chest and Cancer Drive. She has helped at the Cherokee Nursing Home and Volunteer Action Center. [What beautiful people they were, giving me so much more than I gave. Our pastor stressed visitation, and I tried to hold to that duty of Christian life.]

"Beauty in nature and flowers have always held a special interest for her, and she enjoyed membership in the local Garden Club. This love of beauty shows in special interests of painting, music and poetry. She loves to read—especially historical novels. [When I had time.] Her hobbies include cooking, sewing—including draperies—china painting, and walking—especially in the woods and on the beach, and meditating." [And I needed a lot of prayer on the run too!]

It was a blessing that our whole family was there around us in those busy times. Bert saw his mother and dad almost every day while we lived in Calhoun. Every day for some forty years. And I tried to do the same for his and my mother. Mrs. Lance and I especailly liked to go shopping in Atlanta, and we went to most of the same church circles together. Those kinds of things are natural when you live close to one another. And we have always been close—in space and in spirit.

But when you have a family the size of ours, you share the hardships intensely along with the happiness. There is sorrow and pain. We lived through a hard time with my mother when she developed breast cancer, nearly ten years ago. Ultimately she had to have a radical mastectomy. And then developed pneumonia and a high fever the very day she was supposed to have had the operation. So the doctors decided to postpone the operation, knowing all along that postponement was dangerous. We took her to Puerto Rico where she basked in lots of sun.

Mother's mental attitude deteriorated. We strained to keep her spirits up. This was long before the days when mastectomies were common and treated with the objectivity and good sense that is so necessary. Women everywhere owe Betty Ford a debt for the courage and sense she demonstrated when she had the operation. It showed women everywhere that they needn't hide nor fear the shock to their femininity. Mother pulled through the pneumonia and then she had the operation which affected her severely afterward. Now she is well past the five-year period which most doctors say is the time in which the cancer will begin to show up again if it is not completely removed. Since her operation Mother has worked actively in the Cancer Society's "Reach for Recovery" program, to help others who faced the same ordeal.

On the whole our lives were tranquil and growing more prosperous throughout the 1950s. Bert advanced to the presidency of the bank in the early 60s and the bank too was expanding. Bert's philosophy as a country banker boiled down to something simple and straightforward: "You have to know a man to trust his business judgment, and you've got to expect to lose a dime to make a dollar." What he meant was that when you are lending money to make a profit on the interest, you've got to take a reasonable risk. Bert believed in taking risks on people, because as a father, a teacher, and a banker, he had learned that if you show someone you believe in him he will do his best. He wasn't the kind of banker who "makes the borrower prove that he doesn't really need the money before he will agree to lend it to him." Bert's greatest satisfaction in his work came when one of his loans turned out well and resulted in the creation of new business and new jobs. He is proud of his part in a farmer's or businessman's success. And with these successes, the bank grew too, and so did Bert's responsibility.

Bert was becoming a success, and he put the emphasis on "becoming." Bert's idea of achievement was that "success is a movable target." He set his goals at the start of his active life, but he kept changing them as he approached them. Success, he believed, was not a matter of ruthless ambition, it's a matter of trying always to do your best for yourself, your family, your friends and your country. Success is a journey, not a destination, he believes. It is important, he feels, always to have something just ahead to strive for. That means you may have to suffer and make some costly mistakes, but it's better to try to live up to your potential than live down to your lowest level of mediocrity. Bert also placed a high value on a good sense of humor. There is no spice in life without it, and no better way to weather life's storms, he believes, than with prayer and laughter. Bert has always seemed to most people to be extremely self-confident. What not everyone recognizes is that it is not ego-confidence; it is a confidence born of self-deprecating humor and the conviction that he is doing what God wants him to do. He prays for guidance before every decision of any importance—but he can laugh at himself if what he *hears* turns out to be what he wants—not what the Lord wants.

"If it ain't broke, don't fix it." In homespun terms that is another maxim describing Bert's attitude toward life and business. He believes in "live and let live," and in the natural working out of a business and personal life. He is not a worrier. When the events of life seem beyond his control, he turns them over to the Lord. His sleep is untroubled. Few of his friends can recall a time when Bert was noticeably angry or distraught. His even temper was matched by his outgoing personality. He was a popular person during his school days, and that continues to be true in his business life. He knows how to work toward a just compromise. I don't know anybody who doesn't like Bert as a person. Maybe there are some who dislike him because of business competition, or who are jealous of him because he is more successful than they are, but Bert takes that in stride and always tries to turn a competitor into a friend and prayer partner.

During his early career, Bert's involvement in civic and business matters was always expanding. North Georgia was a depressed area for many years. The boll weevils in the 1920s, the Depression in the 30s, and the War in the 40s all drove people off the farms, and the ecomony was in a long slump. It really was Bert's generation of bankers and businessmen that began to bring the area back to life again through nurturing the textile industry.

One of the truly innovative programs that originated here in North Georgia, and has had national significance, is the banding together of several counties into a regional planning and development district. Our counties are small and poor and because of this they lacked negotiating power. In order to apply more power—and to apply for federal money and make their voice heard—thirteen counties and thirty-nine municipalities banded together into the Georgia Mountains Planning and Development District in the mid 1960s. Since then, well over twenty million dollars in federal funds for water and sewer facilities, health care clinics, parks and roads has come into North Georgia. This money not only helped create immediate jobs, but the programs created the vital facilities and services that industry demands. Roads, water and sewer systems were absolutely necessary to attract new business. In the first five years of the district's operation, employment grew by 20 percent.

There were twenty-six board members of the District; they were local elected officials. Bert served various roles in District programs. It was ironic that it was an order from the federal Office of Management and Budget in 1971 requiring federal departments and agencies to channel their aid to people through local development districts that revitalized our region. Little did Bert suspect then that he would head the OMB just six years later.

The real value in human terms of this governmental policy was that it put power into the hands of the people. Government agencies which previously had been accustomed to a more autonomous and authoritative style had to have local approval from a given area. This assured that federal funds and loans suited local needs and fitted into an overall regional plan for ecology and development. Bert was personally concerned not only with attracting business but with preserving the natural beauty of northern Georgia for future generations. Tourism also was growing, so our land, lakes, rivers, needed to be protected from exploitation.

It was at one of these regional political meetings in 1966 that Bert first met Jimmy Carter at an outdoor barbeque. It was the kind of country political meeting with speeches that is a Georgia institution. A young state senator named Carter was one of the speakers. After the meeting, Bert went up to talk to him. Picnic tables were set up under the live oak trees and the food was being served out in the open. Bert was attracted initially by Jimmy's forthright approach and community conscience. In private conversation they soon learned that they had much in common besides a broad concern for progress in Georgia. Both of them were raised in a small town, Jimmy in the flatlands of southwest Georgia, and Bert in the hills of the north. Both felt a strong commitment to public service. Both had had boyhood dreams of going to sea. Bert had wanted to go to the Naval Academy as a boy, and Jimmy had gone to the Academy. Both were involved in agri-business, Jimmy as a farmer and warehouser of peanuts, Bert as the financial underwriter. And most important, both felt a strong kinship as born-again Christians with similar principles and goals.

At the first meeting Jimmy disclosed his plans to run for governor. Bert liked him and, though he had not been much involved in state politics or political campaigns, Bert said that he would be glad to do whatever he could for Carter in North Georgia. That was the beginning of a long association that grew into firm friendship and a working partnership in public service.

The beginning, of course, was not overly auspicious.

Jimmy ran long and hard for the governorship but placed third in a six way race in the Democratic primary, behind Ellis Arnall and Lester Maddox, who was the eventual winner of the governor's seat. This defeat precipitated a personal crisis for Jimmy that led to a deep religious experience and a renewed commitment to serve the people of his state.

Jimmy, in a sense, spent the next four years running for the governorship. He made 1,800 speeches and personally met 600,000 Georgians in those four years of campaigning. Jimmy didn't try to carry his message to the people only over TV—he was out at the gates of factories at five in the morning, and there again at midnight to meet and greet the workers as the shifts changed. He was out in the peanut fields at dawn and in the cotton fields at dusk. (We took a leaf from his book when we were on the campaign trail.) Jimmy's grass roots campaign was calculated to speak to and for, as he put it, "the formerly silent people who are not ecomonic or political or social leaders." He wanted all the people of Georgia to know that he would be their candidate and their voice for change and growth in Georgia.

Bert and I both played a somewhat larger part in Jimmy's second run for the governorship, though neither of us served in any official capacity on the campaign staff. We hosted the Carters in Calhoun, and both Jimmy and Rosalynn stayed with us on several occasions while campaigning in and around Gordon County. Bert introduced Jimmy to church and community leaders in our area and worked personally for him locally.

I greatly admired the Carters. I think they taught and inspired me and Bert with a whole new attitude toward Christian stewardship. Jimmy's emphasis on doing one's best arises out of the call to serve one's neighbor that he hears in the Gospel. And though Bert and I had always tried to live by the principle ourselves, we had not realized that our neighbors could be served and their needs met through public service. Even so, neither Bert nor I entertained any idea of going into politics just then. Bert was much involved in managing the growth of the bank in Calhoun, and so he was totally surprised when he got a call after Jimmy's election to serve as the head of the Highway Department. The job was not one in which Bert had obvious experience. But Jimmy had campaigned on the promise of bringing better management and business practices to government, and Bert did have skills in those areas. Jimmy had particularly addressed the problems in the administration of the Highway Department which had been under the control of one man since the 1930s. Federal and state funds for highways, he charged, had become one of the chief pork barrels of political patronage in the state. The whole department, he believed, needed restructuring and cleaning up. So it was obviously an important position that he was asking Bert to take over.

The family discussed it, and Bert and I looked at it from the point of view of family finances. We decided that he ought to take the job, but only if the board of directors of the bank would let him continue on salary in a somewhat more limited capacity of employment. He would in essence be holding down two demanding jobs. We also decided that since his job was for the people, his state salary should be given back to the people. When he took the job we donated his $25,000 Highway Department income to charity.

Bert had always encouraged bank personnel to take part in civic work and public service. He felt that he could not now refuse to do what he urged others to do.

I guess I'm a realist—or maybe just housewife practical. But I couldn't see Bert's qualifications for the highway job at first. Later that day, on our way to a dinner meeting in Rome, Georgia, some thirty miles from Calhoun, we were still talking about the appointment.

"What good do you think *you* could do in the Department?" I asked.

"Well, Jimmy wants to reorganize the state bureaucracies—you know that was one of his chief campaign promises—and I think I can help with that. I've had to manage considerable growth and change in the bank," Bert said.

"But what do you know about building highways?"

"Nothing. But I do know something about people and money and about federal funding. And that's the big problem. Georgia's not getting its fair share of federal money, nor is the money it gets being spent in the right places in the most cost effective manner. The Governor has asked me to mainly be responsible for reorganizing the Department—I hope that means I can make this a temporary job. I can't afford to leave the bank."

It was just about then that we hit a big pothole in the road which almost jarred me out of my seat. It was the main road between the two towns.

"Do you think you could get this 'back road' fixed?" I grumbled.

"That, Darling, will be my number-one priority," he said. And we both laughed.

It was a good way to start a new turn in our life—because we soon discovered that it was not to be all joy and laughter. Nothing is more personally demanding than public life. But nothing can be more rewarding. Nothing more grueling. Progress comes so slowly. That road we drove to Rome, for instance, is still not fixed. It's a unique kind of service and stewardship.

I think sometimes of the story of the Good Samaritan. Usually we see the story from the victim's point of view. We sympathize with him. We are amazed and ashamed at the inhumanity shown him by the three supposedly good religious citizens. We are relieved when the Samaritan, an outsider, takes pity on him. Seen from the Samaritan's point of view the story looks quite different. Shouldn't we sympathize with him? Here's a person taking on a thankless task. He doesn't even know if the wounded man will survive. He's giving his own time, effort and substance to care for another human being. And the Samaritan remains nameless with no rewards or publicity. He is not even thanked. I came to identify many of the wonderful people in public service as the Samaritan people. Many are anonymous, laboring long hours for the public good. I loved the people I met who selflessly served the state of Georgia. Their service has its own rewards.

We started off government service with all the pleasurable and prestigious events. Jimmy Carter's inauguration was quite a thrill with many balls and parties, and for a while we were caught up in a fashionable swirl. Our friends the J. B. Langfords (whose daughter Judy later married Jack Carter) gave a party for Bert and me and invited several notables including the Carters and Governor Robert Scott of North Carolina. It was held at a hotel in Atlanta, and about twenty-four people attended. With his usual attention to detail Jimmy Carter looked over the seating arrangements and changed some of the place cards to create a more congenial table. Both he and Bert were detail-minded. Both were conscious of appearance. Both were attentive to dress. Bert often buys lovely dresses for me.

Bert soon found that running the Highway Department, with some 8000 employees and years of bureaucratic routine built into it, was not an easy task. He remarked that in banking you can see the immediate effects of your decisions. In government you often have to wait years. Especially where highways are concerned. Everyone wants good highways to travel, but not in *their* neighborhood. And the federal, civic, environmental complexities are manifold. The paperwork and red tape are unbelievable.

When Bert took office, one major highway, interstate I-75, had already been approved and in construction since 1965. But one vital link near Atlanta, between Marietta and Adairsville, was still incomplete. The final route was still being bitterly contested. Public groups and environmental impact studies were holding up completion of the highway. The debate raged over which was the best route—over or around Lake Allatoona. The road was finally completed in December 1977.

Bert did not leave Calhoun for the office in Atlanta at 5:45 A.M. solely out of devotion to duty—he also claimed that was the only way to beat the tremendous traffic jam caused by outmoded roads and I-75's incompletion.

Bert is as ecologically concerned as anyone, but he also has a businessman's good sense about getting the best job done for the money. Sometimes he was utterly frustrated by federal red tape. One story he tells is about the time a

highway proposal was turned down because no environmental impact study had been done on the installation of a
bell ringing railroad crossing signal! Imagine! That's not only
foolish—the delay endangered many lives.

Bert found that Governor Carter had need of him in other
ways as well. Bert has just the talent and personality necessary to make people work toward effective compromise, and
he helped steer a gasoline tax package through the legislature which would raise a levy on gasoline to pay for road
improvements. This success led the governor to make Bert
one of his chief "lobbyists" for governmental reorganization, in which scores of state offices and agencies were
integrated into larger departments to increase productivity
and management effectiveness. Bert's own department, for
instance, became the Department of Transportation and he
had the oversight of all forms of mass transportation.

But Bert's other chief success was the job that Jimmy
Carter had hired him for—to eliminate pork barrel politics
and the paying of political favors with highway construction
contracts, and to restore public trust and confidence in the
Department. Bert labored long and hard in a public relations
effort to convince citizens of the impartiality of the Department. But he did more than talk. When the state legislature
passed a law allocating the spending of highway funds
equally among all Georgia's congressional districts, Bert took
that law a step further. He extended equal allocation to other
transportation expenditures like the rural road program, the
bridge building program and county contracts (the most
politically sensitive, because often these repair contracts
came under fire as being politically motivated). The *Atlanta
Constitution* reported that the attitude of the Highway Department had changed from a "can't do" or "what can you
do for *me*"attitude to a "can do" and "what can we do for
you" attitude. This change was a direct extension of Bert's
own personality and vision.

Our lives at this time took on a hustle we could not have
imagined. Bert was spending twelve to sixteen hours a day
on business. I was bouncing from Calhoun to Atlanta. I was
becoming an expert highway commuter too. I was taking

care of four "homes" now, our house and farm, Lancelot, in
Calhoun, an apartment in Atlanta, and a summer home on
Sea Island which we purchased in 1970.

But the most important event in our lives during this
early period of state service was Tram's wedding in 1972.
While attending Georgia State University, Tram fell in love
with Patricia DeWitt. Patty was a lovely girl and we were so
pleased. Tram must have heard me talk about our wedding a
thousand times over the years, but yet I was happily surprised when they said they wanted to duplicate our ceremony. Patty even wore my bridal gown, and they were
married on the same day as Bert and I, September 9.

Finally it had happened—one of my own had flown the
nest. What I had worried so much about finally happened.
And miraculously I found it not hard at all—but a blessing. I,
who had four sons, now had a daughter to love and enjoy. I
had lost nothing, and gained so much more. It filled my
heart with pride and joy to see my son as a young man
stepping off on his own. I too had grown—I could let go. Life
is like that—we learn what we must—and often it is not as
hard as we fear.

Bert's handling of departmental and Carter administration affairs won him many friends and gained him considerable public recognition. So it was at Jimmy Carter's suggestion and firm backing that he made his decision to run for
governor, and in early 1973 he resigned from office to launch
his campaign. In Georgia, a governor cannot serve consecu-
tive terms, so in 1974 Jimmy Carter would be out after four
years. Bert shared Jimmy's vision of a renovated and revived
Georgia, and he wanted to help mold that future on his own.
With much encouragement from Carter supporters Bert
began his campaign.

Jimmy had hopes of higher office. One time on a trip Bert
had picked up a copy of a book in a Chicago airport on
Presidential character and had passed it on to Jimmy. Another time at a party we gave for the Carters, he presented
Jimmy with a set of small medals of all the states, saying he
now had dominion over one—someday he hoped he would
have dominion over all. It was natural for these two kindred

My mother and father in front of Mount Vernon

Me at about age six, playing the part of an angel in the Christmas pageant

Bert and I, teenage sweethearts

Me as a young student,
at Agnes Scott College

Our whole family taken during Bert's campaign for Governor. Stuart, David, Beverly, Patty, and Tram, Bert and me

President Carter and me

Trey, our first grandson, the proud parents Patty and Tram, the beaming grandmother and grandfather

President-elect Carter with Walter Mondale, Rosalynn Carter, Bert, me and Mrs. and Mr. Cyrus Vance

Bert reading opening statement to the Senate Governmental Affairs Committee

Meeting at St. Simons Island, with Michael Blumenthal, Bert, President-elect Carter, Charles Schultze, Walter Mondale

Scene in the hearing room before the Senate Governmental Affairs Committee

David, me, Dr. and Mrs. Chance at Senate hearings

spirits to think big, seek the highest, and do their best. For Jimmy that meant a two-year quest for the Presidency; for Bert it meant a two-year quest for the governorship of the state of Georgia.

It was a bit more difficult to convince me about this run for office. My family background had not been in politics but in business. I already knew the rigors of public life—where one is criticized and under the scrutiny of the press, the public, and political opponents. Bert had been attacked by a few people for conflict of interest in holding both his job at the bank and in the Highway Department—even though he stated it was but temporary service to reorganize the Department.

Finally it took a word from Rosalynn Carter to change my mind. She said that Christians must seek to serve—and that "seeking" was as difficult as "serving," but just as necessary. One must strive to do his best and utmost. I admired her spirit and willingness to give herself, and I agreed to help all I could with Bert's run for the Governor's chair.

We announced Bert's candidacy at a party held out at Lancelot, at which Bert spoke from the bed of an old wagon to friends and guests presenting the major themes of his candidacy. He was, commentators were to say later, to take the "high road" in politics. He did not attack fellow candidates. He did not engage in political factionalism, exploit racial fears, or blare out apocalyptic warnings. He called on citizens to help him serve all the people and the state. The slogan for his campaign was "I need your help." It was an invitation to bring more people into responsive dialogue with their government.

Several things impressed professional political commentators about Bert's style. This quote from Hal Gulliver's column in the June 17, 1974 edition of the *Atlanta Constitution* tells what they liked about him and also gives a pretty good picture of a typical campaign day:

". . . Lance flew out of Calhoun in north Georgia in time to make a news conference on the courthouse square in Bainbridge in deep southwest Georgia, got interviewed there by two bright radio station men, went around the square to have coffee with former Governor Marvin Griffen who ain't supporting anybody but who likes to tell a story or two and introduce visiting candidates to the "shadetree philosophers" also drinking coffee, toured Bainbridge, then later to Whigham and Climax and Cairo and Pelham, and after flying out of south Georgia, to Walton County and Monroe for a little campaigning and a civic club speech."

Mr. Gulliver concluded by saying, "It's early, there's a lot to come. But there aren't many candidates in any race that cover as much territory, shake as many hands, make as many contacts and run it all on some kind of planned schedule as Bert Lance manages to do."

I remember so many days like that. The campaign was going well. We lived like nomads for almost two years, and every day brought another major event. Campaigning is an exercise in capturing the public attention.

I remember the day Bert opened his Atlanta campaign headquarters on Peachtree Street. There was the usual crowd of supporters. Banners were hung in the windows. (One large one asking "What have *they* done for you lately?" "They," being the professional politicians who were doing business as usual. Bert was campaigning on performance and a positive attitude about the future of the state.) There were several college students dressed up in costumes including one dressed as Snoopy. It's hard to attract a crowd even with all this paraphernalia, so when a rock group started playing in a park across the street at lunchtime Bert went across to where people were. He was always going to where the people were. So were we all.

We walked in so many parades I could have run the Boston Marathon. We always walked together, Bert and I. Usually Bert would hold my hand, because I'm quite nearsighted and in a crowd I get easily lost, but also because we considered this business to be "ours." The whole family joined in. We were apart frequently as a family, but we were all together in spirit—all for one and one for all in this enterprise. Tram and Pattyopened Bert's Bibb County campaign headquarters in Macon when he was not able to attend, and all the boys took part in various ways.

David traveled all over to talk with youth groups; Stuart

spent days stuffing envelopes and helping at headquarters.

Campaigns have both sublime and ridiculous moments. Times when the response from the crowd is so good you feel like you're walking on air. And times when the response is so bad or so flat it feels like the air has been drained out of the meeting hall. Our schedule was so tight we'd be leaving a very formal reception heading for a rural tent-meeting-style gathering and changing clothes en route. Many times I ate at McDonald's dressed to the teeth in a long gown and jewels. It was a real circus—full of fun and absurdity, but with a serious purpose and serious consequences for our state.

Sometimes Bert and I traveled separately, but we always made it a point to stay together each night, even if it were at no place more homey than another chain motel. But we were each other's best friend and confidant, and we shared all our triumphs and frustrations and helped massage the fatigue from one another's weary bodies and souls. Bert was suffering from back trouble, a ruptured disc, during the whole campaign. He was in severe pain, though no one in the crowd would know it by his verve and enthusiasm. Sometimes he had to sleep sitting up in a lounge chair. Sometimes he couldn't sleep at all. Yet every morning he was up early and off on the campaign trail again.

As time drew closer to the August 13 Democratic primary, the election heated up with a series of charges exchanged among the major candidates—an exchange that Bert avoided. The strategy of all the hopefuls was at first to put their efforts against Lt. Governor (and Governor before Jimmy Carter) Lester Maddox, who was running for re-election to the Governor's seat and was by far the best-known person in the field. It soon became evident that with a crowded field of candidates a runoff was likely. A second place finish was to be as important as a first, since no one would get an outright majority. Lester Maddox seemed to have a firm hold on the more conservative vote, and Bert and State House majority leader George Busbee were the primary recipients of the more liberal, urban and black vote.

Bert was running on his record of successes in the Highway Department and as a candidate who stood for the continuation of Jimmy Carter's progressive policies. The other major issues of the campaign did not have much impact. But in the final days of the campaign, after Bert had revealed his campaign financing and personal wealth, some of the other candidates tried to fasten on him the negative image of "rich man." Bert did in fact spend as much money as the other candidates, and spent more of his own money. But that we hoped would be seen as not making him beholden to other individuals or particular interest groups.

On July 28th we hosted a country picnic for 2,500 friends and supporters at our farm Lancelot. It was, in a way, the high water mark of the campaign. Commentators said later that Bert "peaked" two weeks too soon. But going into election eve he was a slight favorite for second place over George Busbee.

Election eve we had dinner at Tram and Patty apartment and then went early to the Executive Park Hotel, in Atlanta, where two thousand campaign workers had crowded into the ballroom. We watched the news and the returns as soon as they started coming in. But at 9 P.M., feeling "antsy," we went down to greet our friends in the ballroom. Bert spoke and then I thanked everyone for their help. Some TV news people asked me for my predictions.

"I'm a realist," I said, "and I'm still going to watch the returns, keep your fingers crossed." But for some reason I had a vague foreboding that it wasn't going to work out.

We had to wait all night because the election was so close. But by the next morning it was clear that Lester Maddox was in first place with well over 200,000 votes, George Busbee had come in second with 105,000 votes, and Bert was third with 95,000. In the primary runoff election Busbee picked up votes that had gone to Bert and others. He defeated Maddox and went on to win the governorship in the general election in November.

With characteristic style and grace, Bert congratulated the victors, and without regrets or a backward glance, he returned to his banking business. I was glad to go home, happy to leave the campaign trail for a quieter, more sedentary life at home. Had it all been for nothing, I wondered. Two years spent walking the back roads and city avenues of

Georgia. No, I guessed it must have a secret purpose that God would reveal in time. I thanked God that he had allowed me this interesting experiment and vital involvement with people and politics of my beloved state. And I went happily home to Calhoun and then to our Sea Island retreat to recharge my exhausted body and spirit.

Sea Island
–an interlude–

When we finally moved into the Sea Island house, I felt we had closed a circle—in some personal sense we had encompassed Georgia. We were both born in the northern highlands at the foot of the Blue Ridge Mountains, we came to young adulthood and to public life in Atlanta and in the Piedmont region, and now we were coming to a place below the Fall Line Hills, rich in all the history which was almost the emblem of fabled old Dixie. Here was the oldest part of Georgia with Spanish moss, old live oaks. Here is beauty and calm! Here the low green coast merges with the warm gray-blue swells of the sea. At low tide the beige Atlantic beaches stretch seamlessly to the pale and distant horizon.

We had been going to the Georgia coastal islands on family vacations for years. When the boys were very young, we'd stay at a motel on Jekyll Island for a few days. In later years, Bert would lease a house at Sea Island for two weeks and the children and I would go down first. Bert would join us for a few days and on weekends. He worked so hard sometimes I worried about him, but he always had boundless energy. He has always worked long and hard but he was not one who lived for his work alone. It was just characteristic of him to throw himself into church work and community services with the same total dedication as on the job. That's the way he spent his family time too. He made the most of it; the quality of the time we spent together had to make up for its brevity.

We were organized in our activity, whether it was family devotions or outings at the beach. Bert liked to see or find extra value in everything. So he'd turn vacations into study times for the boys. If we went on vacation we would always read about the places we were touring—New York, Washington, Europe. If we went to the "Golden Isles" along Georgia's coast, it was an opportunity to learn something about the geography, history and customs of our own state. I was always collecting brochures for the boys, directing side trips to historical buildings and markers, and reading some of the old accounts of the explorers and planters. Sometimes the boys grew tired of museums, cathedrals, or plantation homes—but at least they carried home something more than a good time.

The Islands are the repository of a long and emblematic history of the South. It was here that the finest long-fiber cotton in the world was grown in the eighteenth and nineteenth centuries. The planters grew rich. They built huge plantation houses constructed of native timber raised on foundations of "tabby," a locally made cement composed of fossil lime and oyster shells. Everything that was needed for their gracious and self-sufficient way of life lay close at hand—the cotton, the timber, the fruits of the sea and slaves.

Fort Fredericka on St. Simon's was an early stockade and lookout post for the Spanish who founded it almost a hundred years before the Pilgrims stepped ashore on their cold and rocky northern shore.

The colonial and pre-Civil War periods were years of prosperity for the islands and coastal Georgia. But when a Union Fleet appeared off St. Helena Island in 1861, the plantation owners retreated inland from their indefensible island and hundreds of slaves volunteered to join the Union forces. The War was the beginning of a long decline for the Islands. It has been only recently that increased tourism, fueled by the mild warm climate, the ocean and its beautiful beaches and the natural beauty of the terrain, has begun to bring change and prosperity to the Islands once again. And the fact that the Islands have become a Presidential retreat also adds to their interest and attraction.

It is strange and marvelous to realize as I walk around the salt marshes, and up and down the level wide beach, drawing spiritual refreshment from the place, that the same God who renews me also works in history to renew lands and peoples. He overturns some structures and societies so that new life can spring forth. How little and weak we are, I realize, beside God's tides—of sea and history.

It was exactly for renewal that we chose to come to Sea Island. After the defeat in the governor's race, we needed a place to come to reassess our goals. It was a place for us to hide away, a place to come to recharge. We had bought our home, "Marshwinds," a pink two story old island house, for just that reason four years before in 1970. Neither Bert nor I had imagined the degree of scrutiny that comes to bear on persons running for office or in public life, nor did we imagine the strain that can accrue from it. Bert always insisted that the public's right to know us, our lives, business and ideas came before personal considerations—that, he said, is simply given, a condition of public service. If you "go public" you owe the public the right of knowing you, its servants, for the season you serve. But on days he had free, what a joy it was to come to Sea Island and to be private, to share and enjoy one another's company without being on public view. It was a place to come for healing. So many sea creatures and birds come to life in the marsh. It is a place of protection before they grow and dare the high winds and seas. I felt like one of them, come to a snug harbor to gather my strength.

Marshwinds is not quite in keeping with the grand resort tradition. It is an older house, on the marsh, bought at a bargain because of water damage. It has no special architecture, it's just comfortable. But I had grown to love it as I decorated it. I put in upholstered furniture in light beige; it has grass cloth walls and other rooms painted green. I wanted to rescue it from neglect and restore it with tender loving care. After eighteen months on the road, sleeping in a different bed every night, meeting people day after day, being always available, trying always to be responsive, to listen intelligently, to hear the personal need and cry in the same questions asked day after day in one meeting hall after another—it was good to come to Marshwinds and be as quiet as the sea at ebb tide.

And our boys too had been under great strain. They were

proud of their father, but they missed him. And they missed
me. How many nights did I go to bed wondering what they
were doing, praying that they were all right. And these were
their difficult teen years. There were drugs and protest and
rebellion of every sort. And our boys were not untouched.
Almost everything others have been through with children,
we have too—school problems, drugs, car accidents, etc.
So Sea Island became our natural sanctuary, a place for
reflection, for getting to know one another again in the quiet
of the natural beauty God had created.

Marshwinds is circled about with many trees. Live oaks
rise from the marsh's edge draped with Spanish moss. There
are palmettos, longleaf pine, magnolias and myrtles, royal
poinciana, wisteria and tea olive in the area. Camellias and
azaleas cover our yard. Flowers grow in wild, natural profusion. I love the small, ever-bearing beauty of the kumquat
tree. The warm, soft air is filled with the fragrances of the
sea, the song of birds and crackle of insects.

These Golden Isles are on the Atlantic Flyway and are the
destination or stopping off place for migrating Canadian
geese and baldpate ducks and hundreds of other species of
birds. The tidal flats of Cape Romain, on the northern head
of the islands, are the largest wildlife refuge on the Atlantic
coast. It is for this profusion of God's bounty that we came
here, and for the peace that God gives. Bert and I love it.
Sometimes the boys want more excitement, but for us, age
has its deepening appreciation of stillness. We have learned
to be quiet and know that he is God. We have learned to
accept beauty as no small gift. We have learned to open our
eyes to it, and open our hearts to it. Beauty teaches us
something essential about ourselves and paradise.

I'd often go for walks by myself around the marsh, or
peddle my bike along the beach or over the wild trails that
skirt the marsh. The silence, except for the wind in the grass
which made the stillness in its pauses even more profound,
seemed to swallow me up. I could smell the sea and the dark
pungent smell of things growing and decaying. I'd move
slowly across the soft, spongy wet sand, watching my foot-
prints fill up with water.

There was a place I especially liked, a sunny spot off our patio amid old bent trees. It was on the edge of the marsh, closed in behind by oak trees. I'd lie in this little shelter on a lounge chair which still offered a view over the marsh. There in the sun and dappled shade I could relax and meditate.

"What have I learned?" I'd ask myself. "What has God taught me? Where do I go from here?" The questions came more easily than the answers. But since I'd experienced most of the shocks to which human flesh is heir, I should have learned something. Listen to the wind. What is it saying? What do the trees know naturally that is so hard for me to hear?

"To trust," I thought. "To accept." I've learned that. I learned that even as a child when my only recourse was to take things one day at a time. Learn to read the changing clouds. That is a child's way. Look at the oak—its strength for the days, how it grows slowly and well, putting down deep roots. A child does not recognize the full scope of a problem as an adult might. She takes the problem one tiny piece at a time as she meets that part of it. If as a child I'd been able to see that Alcoholism with a capital "A" was my family's problem, I wouldn't have been able to cope. But I faced the symptoms day by day and survived. I grew in knowledge. Later when my mother gave me a word from God about my father's death, she released me immediately from fear and doubt. A child trusts and accepts. An adult becomes more able on her own to cope, but perhaps is less trusting. I had to learn to keep the trust of a child. That is how Jesus wanted us to come to him.

It's the simplest things that adults forget. Things that nature knows. Things that even an infant knows intuitively. A child eats when it's hungry. Adults eat even when they are full, or they forget to eat when their stomachs are empty. They get too nervous to eat. Or they eat when they are nervous. We are preoccupied with the world. For years, for example, I'd skip breakfast because I had no time for it. My mother would scold me, tell me I couldn't keep up with a troop of energetic boys if I didn't have energy myself. "Eat breakfast," she'd say. And I'd laugh and respond, "With so many 'energetic' boys, who has time for breakfast?" A small thing, but who does have the time?

Time is all we have. Our bodies are all we have. Sometimes, sitting on the terrace wall, I could see birds walking cautiously through the marsh grass, looking out for food and for enemies. Their whole lives are occupied in this way. Yet their pace was a natural unfolding of circumstance—they were not rushed. They existed in a time that flowed through them and through all things around them—and not upon some rushed and private timetable. A bird turned its head and looked at me for the longest time, and then went step, step, fly.

It was only when I reached my forties that I learned to eat wisely once again. Maybe the boys were old enough to fend for themselves and give me a chance to turn back to concerns about myself. Maybe I just got around finally to listening to Mother's advice. It's always a matter of having ears to hear. Before I'd go for my walks by the marsh, I'd eat a good breakfast of eggs and toast or cereal, and milk and coffee, and juice. And I was always surprised how light and lively I'd feel. How content to sit on some fallen log, pleasantly full but not stuffed. How different I felt from times when I'd eat and run.

As nutritional philosophy, eating well and wisely is only common sense. But as theology it has a deeper meaning. The Bible tells us our bodies are the temple of God's spirit. What does it mean to live in a body not cared for? How many of us would take as poor care of our house as we do of ourselves? Let the inside paint peel, the floors get scuffed up, the appliances go on the blink, the windows become dirty? A house like that is potentially dangerous. It breaks down and falls apart. It is a catastrophe caused by sloth or greed or gluttony. And a body treated similarly makes the spirit coarse, sluggish, torpid, subject to vices, and liable to spiritual accidents and indulgences. A wise person builds upon sound principles—faith, nutrition, discipline—as the man in the parable built his house upon solid rock.

I read somewhere that you should eat breakfast like a king, lunch like a prince, and supper like a pauper. Controlling appetite is the key to discipline—physical as well as spiritual discipline. And, in fact, the two are related—because the condition of the body often reflects the condition of our minds and in some cases our souls. If we are open and willing, God will take care of our undernourished spirits, and a fully nourished spirit eliminates the problem of hungry desires.

Everything has a lesson if we have ears to hear the message. Birds can be singing all around me in the marsh, and if I'm absorbed in my own gloom, I don't hear them, only the thump of a somber muffled tune, the drugged song of my heart. In fact, all nature is singing. Do you take time to hear it?

Grief? I've had to learn grief, bereavement, abandonment in a dozen different ways in my life. I saw a muskrat nosing the dead body of one of its offspring that must have wandered from its burrow. It sniffed and walked away. How casual and cruel, I thought. And then it hit me that grief was a blessing. We can feel. Thank God, we can feel! We do not turn our back on suffering, and we keep memories alive as witness to the souls of those we loved. It hurts, but what an exquisite hurt it is. What a blessing in disguise. We neither planned nor can remember our birth—isn't that a mystery as profound as death? We do not recollect our birth with fear; why should we then fear death which God has planned for us? His love encompasses both.

When Granddaddy died in 1952, I went about my business. I took care of arrangements. I helped Grandmother and Mother at the dinner afterward. I set the table and put out the silver, and poured coffee and tea. By nature I react calmly and quietly at the moment of greatest stress and starkest separation. I hold it all in, not only for myself, but for others. There are others grieving as well, and at a time like that you have to show compassion. You have to show some control so others can hold life together. Someone may need you more than you need tears. You sacrifice your strength for those who need it most. Then I cry my eyes out later. Fastening a buckle of my shoe, I remember how Granddaddy did it for me when I was a child. "Let's get on to church,

Honey," he'd say. "We don't want to be late for Sunday school." Then I'd cry, flooded with memories of his goodness and sensations of my loss. Bert comforted me. He held me in his arms until the tears ebbed and carried away the hurt. He was my rock in this terrible time.

My family looks at me and says, "I thought she was OK." And I tell them, "Now I will be." I have to work it out first and cry it out later. And the solace in tears brings a purgation of emotion and a release and all the rest is with God.

In quietness and calmness you find strength. Sometimes staring out over my marsh, I think of Moses and the Israelites—how God led them all the way through forty years of blistering desert, every kind of wilderness of rock and stone, and sin and hardness of the spirit, and brought them to the very verge of the Promised Land. In trial they learned forebearance, and in solitude they gained strength. At last they had grown enough to pass over into the Promised Land without Moses, and he went to a better land than they.

God has taught me in this fashion. He has surrounded me with love and beauty all the days of my life. From the springs and creeks and hills around Calhoun, to the man-made beauty of polished steel, stone and glass in Atlanta, to the soft earth tones and water colors of the sand and marsh and sea here at Sea Island.

And his quiet comfort and beauty and assurance has been sufficient to carry me through all the times of trouble as well. He readies each of us for the next step. He is like a parent always holding out his arms to a toddler. If you try, if you dare to take that step, he will catch you. So that in this life you walk step by awkward step toward a total trusting relationship with God. You can get to a point where in everything you can depend on him—whether it be emotional exhaustion, or bankruptcy or terminal cancer. And whatever situation you find yourself in, he can give you peace in it. Therein lies the secret of living—the blessing of faith.

I'm a wife and mother. There are many other things that I do, roles that I play, but my husband and children come first. The hardest thing for a wife and mother is to learn how to let go of the ones she loves—to allow them breathing room, room to grow. That is true for a wife who feels the competition from her husband's job. It is true for a mother who fears her children's growing up and leaving the nest. It is only in letting go that one may hold onto the essential part—hold on to love. If you try to hold on to a butterfly, you crush it. A mother who allows her son to grow up does not lose a son, she gains the love and respect of an independent young man. It is one of those difficult paradoxes that the Lord teaches us—we have to lose a life to gain it. Difficult, hard and painful to learn. But true and necessary. I've always heard the saying, "When children are little they step on your toes—when they are grown they step on your heart." It's true, and it's sometimes necessary. Both child and parent grow through pain.

When a child becomes a teen the rending is most severe. All along that tiny bundle of a baby is exercising his "No." He is saying, "I am not you." At first it is cute or naughty—but not too serious. He also stretches himself. The toddler wants to run before he can walk; the child wants to climb to the treetops but can't tie his climbing shoes, the boy wants to be a superhero but is shy in school—all this is a proper exercise of will and of dreams. If our reach didn't exceed our grasp we wouldn't be human, wouldn't be worthy of God's special care.

But when a child becomes a teen his physical ability is no longer limited. He seems almost a man, and is, *almost*. His power to do himself harm is tremendous, because his desires are all short ranged and not fully under the control of reason. He still wants the instant gratification, approval and success that a child wants. Most teenagers are not grown emotionally, not totally trained up by the Lord. And the dangers are so great. I think of the three "D's" that can lead to death: Drinking, Driving and Drugs. The three "S's" that can lead to a tarnished soul; Sex, Self-indulgence and Sin. The three "R's"—Rage, Rashness, Ridicule that can lead to rejection of parents and God. There are so many dangers. And I have seen them all. All parents have. How can we cope? How can we open the eyes that are not yet able to see?

How can we penetrate the ears that do not want to hear?

The Lord has taught me one lesson—you do your best all along and then you turn your children loose. I do not mean turn them *out*. I mean *loose*—lighten the reins of control and authority and as you do, you must in your own soul turn them over to God. The Lord who sees each sparrow, surely sees your child. Can't he do a better job than you? Our job as parents is to do as Proverbs 22:6 says, "Train up a child in the way he should go: and when he is old he will not depart from it." When he is old he will have himself and God to rely on.

With man all things are impossible, with God all things are possible. When I've heard that idea discussed in Bible class it usually is talked about in the context of "Things that I want"—a job, success, money, healing. I can't do it, but if I pray enough, the attitude seems to be, God will do it or get it for me. But I think of that notion in another way—how would I be able to get through a single day without God? God makes possible the difficult problems of coping with life. Or another example: a friend of mine and I were talking about a woman we know who is divorced.

"Why doesn't she go out and get a job?" my friend said. "She'd be so much better off. A lot of women do it."

I commented, "Maybe she wants to spend more time with her children, and she has a busy schedule now. Could you handle both a job and rearing children?"

For some people it is impossible to speak in public. For others diving off the high board is impossible. For me the thought of "losing" my family used to be *impossible*. But God can get us through, get us over, help us cope with the impossible task of being human. Those are the things "impossible with man," the things we cannot do on our own that are at the limits of our reason, our reach, our talent, our physical or emotional strength. But with God, we can do what we cannot do on our own. We can even do what we "ought" instead of doing the very thing we ought not to do, and even do not want to do, as Paul teaches us. A good friend of mine puts it this way, "Life is full of *oughtas*, *gottas*, and *wantas*. Just make sure you have them in that order." With God's help we can.

This is a stage like adolescence. Self control is a problem for teenagers. They are frequently so caught up in the surges of their will, so awash with emotions that they do the very thing they do not want. Confronted by the limits of their powers, some turn and flee into desperation, indulgence, delusion or aimlessness. At this stage drugs are so seductive not only because of peer-pressure, but because they produce a lessening of conflict and tension. They quiet the rages of the will, but only into a blank vegetative silence.

When Bert and I were on the campaign trail for almost two years, it did indeed have an effect on our boys. As closely as our boys were supervised, we knew that the mere fact that we were away could make them feel that they were on their own. Naturally others, even family, would be more reticent or reluctant to rebuke them for bad behavior or admonish them to do their best. So we made it a strict rule: whether we are home or not, you must act as if we were. We are your parents, we will support you, defend you, but you must be answerable for what you do. We had a long-running discussion over many months about drugs, which are a problem in every school in the country. City ghetto or rural village—drugs are there. What a horrible shame. Our children are being poisoned with lies and then poison themselves with the fruit of these lies.

Our word to the boys was strict. We cannot be liberal-minded or tolerant about what we feel is a threat to the life and happiness of our children. We told them that if they were caught with drugs they must pay the penalty—the full legal penalty. The law was the law. If you break the drug law or any other law you must be accountable for your actions.

You can imagine—or if you have teens you know—what these edicts from Mom and Dad are like. Oh! the Socratic (and not so Socratic) arguments we had. Would parents ever be enlightened? Why is the older generation so . . . so old? I'm afraid there were many times when communication broke down—not just over this problem, but a dozen others. And worse, there were times when we seemed to be drifting far away from each other. How strange to see your children passing like strangers through your life. Those very ones whose bottoms you powdered and noses you wiped—all of a sudden, tall, gangling, shaggy-haired strangers. We had to give them up to God—the one to whom they would never be strangers. Lectured-out, cried-out, I had to give control over to God because I had lost control.

Ultimately we were rewarded, as parents sometimes are. Those we let go are coming back to us. At times I wondered if the Prodigal would be lost forever. There was one point when a breach seemed unbridgeable and the situation impossible. I felt that I had given a child up for dead. And it was not just my pain that hurt—but his pain, his confusion, his thralldom to a perverse will that nearly broke our hearts. But God was with him. And with us. And if they live, children will grow. Thank God he grew.

It was good to be together again as a family here by the sea! I listened for changes in the wind, and watched the waves roll forever in.

Atlanta

After the campaign was over, we had one of those "openings" that God sometimes brings into our lives. If he closes one door, he often opens another. If he seems to close all the doors, he opens a window.

We had a short pause. Something major had just come to an end—18 months of traveling, talking, and politicking. Now it was over. What was next? The treadmill had stopped and we got off and asked, what do we really want to do? What does God want us to do? Some people called our election try a defeat. It was, of course, a disappointment to us, but life is full of those and we hoped it might contain some secret blessing. For some people the treadmill never stops. You work in a factory or an office and you just go on and on until you retire. Then you ask yourself, "What have I done with my life? Where did it go?"

But God stopped the treadmill for us. He closed doors and opened windows. We took a deep breath and looked around, looked outside ourselves for what seemed like the first time in nearly two years.

We had debts. They had to be paid. That meant we needed a good income. We had a family that greatly needed our attention. Our boys were growing teens experiencing some personal traumas. That meant we had to find something stable, a job that would allow us to stay in one place. And as we were standing there looking around, listening for God's word, waiting for just the right things, Bert got an offer from the National Bank of Georgia. It was an old, prestigious institution, much larger than Calhoun First National, but one that needed to break out of old patterns and grow. The bank wanted a new president who was an optimistic go-getter, a man who was expansive and known to the public. If the campaign had done nothing else it had certainly made Bert's face and name well-known in every city and hamlet across the state. The job fit all our requirements, and it seemed to come so unexpectedly—blowing in through the only open window—that we felt sure it was God's will for us at that time. Atlanta was already like a second home to us. Bert accepted.

We continued to stay in our Atlanta apartment temporarily. Tram was working, and David was going to school at Emory—both in Atlanta. Stuart and Beverly wanted to stay in Calhoun and finish school there, so we arranged to have an old family friend take care of them. And we arranged to commute as often as possible between Atlanta and Calhoun.

I started looking for a larger, more permanent place to live. At first I looked at larger apartments. In Atlanta there are so many beautiful condominiums with spectacular views from high rise buildings that I was attracted to them at first. But after looking at several I began to long for a house, something with a bit more space and privacy. If only I could find something in the Atlanta area that had the soul of our house at Sea Island or a feeling of the hill country. I had always loved two-story colonials, so I looked especially for those.

In April, 1975, I went on a house tour which was to raise money for Atlanta's symphony orchestra. The flowers were beginning to bloom, the delicate onset of spring filled the air. Houses which recalled the history and grandeur of the old South were opened to us.

There was one house that was vacant, Mayfair, a large classic colonial mansion in a northern suburb of Atlanta, in which designers and decorators were showing the best of their collections and creations. When the bus pulled through the stone pillars of this elegant mansion, I felt a shock of recognition. It was as if my girlhood fantasies of the house I wanted to build had become reality right before my eyes. It was even bigger than I had dreamed. It was lovely, huge, but delicately symmetrical, with a formal Georgian front entrance with four columns and in back a Mount Vernon porch with eight columns.

A distinguished Southern house built in the 1920s, it had since been renovated, air conditioned and improved by subsequent owners. I had seen it empty once before, but at first it didn't enter my mind to buy it. I imagined it was far too expensive. Several months passed before I learned that it was on the market. Still it didn't seem possible that we could afford a sixty-room house. But then I learned it was being sold on the court house steps because of bankruptcy. I asked Bert to take a look at it with a real estate agent, and he too loved the dignified house. He made inquiries and discovered it was soon to be put up for auction by the city courts. We discussed the matter and decided to make a minimal offer. Our bid was turned down, but we discovered that ours had been the highest.

I went on looking at other places. It was a joy to explore Atlanta's fine old neighborhoods; there were so many lovely homes. But in comparison with Mayfair all other houses dimmed—they were too small and too expensive for what they offered.

I was beginning to become a bit downhearted, when late in summer the city clerk notified us that the house was still unsold and bidders were being contacted again to see if they would renegotiate their bids. I was ecstatic. Somehow I was sure this was meant for us. I talked to Bert; he checked our finances and made our maximum bid. It was the only bid, and it was accepted. I felt a huge sense of relief, a sense of joy, a feeling of rightness about the purchase. It had to come from God; otherwise how could it have been exactly what I had been dreaming of, on the market for so long, purchasable at just the right price? Here was a home that would suit all our needs. We could keep our children and our children's children in it. Bert could use it for entertaining clients and business friends. It would be a house that would reestablish our family in Atlanta and give foundation to a new life together.

I rechristened the house "Butterfly Manna." Butterflies

had a special personal meaning ever since Granddaddy took me walking through the fields as a child. To me they represent beauty and grace and light and wonderful freedom. And when I discovered that the butterfly was a Christian symbol of new life, of resurrection and immortality, I felt an even deeper significance in this personal symbol of joy.

"Manna," of course, is the gift that falls from heaven directly from God's bounty and goodness. It is the bread that fed the children of Israel on their journey to the Promised Land every day. The two words, "Butterfly Manna," precisely expressed my feeling about this house—it was a gift from God, a gift of beauty and joy in which we would find a new start, a new life.

From the beginning we felt very much at home in the house. There's a rocky stream that runs through the property; it's a little touch of north Georgia. A country place in the midst of the city, and only fifteen minutes from the bank where Bert worked. The natural trees and plantings are beautiful; they enclose the house and create a separate place. I planted a butterfly garden down below, between the house and the stream. It's surrounded by azaleas and there are rose bushes planted in the shape of a cross. Bert and I wanted to have a tennis court—we all play tennis—so we put in a court on the lower side near the stream.

Our neighbors were wonderful. Mrs. Lowance from across the street came over with fresh baked bread (a true gift of manna) and everyone made us feel so much at home, we felt we were being greeted by "country neighbors." When we first moved in, I loved to walk around the neighborhood for exercise. There is a beautiful, wooded feel about the area. And wonderful varieties of plants and flowers—especially roses, camellias and azaleas—were everywhere.

I began laying plans for painting and decorating our new home. My brother Barker is quite artistic and has a fine eye for detail, color and arrangement. He volunteered to help me redecorate the house. We did much of the work ourselves. We must have tried every chair in at least ten places. Barker is very meticulous and precise. He has a good hand for corners and trim. He can pick out where to hang the paintings, and judge if they are hung straight.

We bought a few pieces of furniture, but for the most part we brought in things we'd inherited, purchased and stored over the years for our dream house. There were a couple of special pieces I'd bought a few years before with a house like this in mind: an elegant French crystal chandelier which we hung in the dining room, several beautiful paintings of the South by Herbert Shuptrine, Charles Adkerson and several other artists, and a gorgeous Chinese rug which we put in the formal dining room, where we kept our large, mahogany inlaid Sheraton table with Chippendale chairs.

The work proceeded easily because I was so happy doing it. It was good to be settling in, good to have our family together again, good to have Bert taking hold at NBG. He was filming a number of TV spots promoting the bank, capitalizing on his recognizability with Georgians. Everything was going well.

When Bert and I decided to move to Atlanta, we started attending church at the Peachtree Road Methodist Church. We had been made so welcome there, had been given so much Christian love and fellowship, that our move had been accomplished with a minimum of emotional strain. I think the image of big cities and city people as cold and uncaring is spread only by those who are not part of a church. Christian fellowship is as warm and deep in the city as it is in the country. How many young people, single people, old and alone people, could be helped out of isolation into the fellowship and intimacy they long for if they would only allow themselves the pleasure and benefit of Christian fellowship. Many large urban churches have growing active groups for every conceivable interest and age grouping—youth fellowships, singles groups, covenant groups for the widowed and bereaved, divorced parents' gatherings, as well as Bible study and Christian women's groups. (This was true in Washington as well as in Atlanta, we later discovered.)

But it began to dawn on me that something more than mere comfortable living was required of my life. God was leading me to discipline. I think he wanted me to work as

hard at putting my spiritual house in order as I did Butterfly
Manna. What did he want, I wondered. I thought a lot about
it as I polished furniture and set out plants and flowers in the
courtyard. Maybe he wanted just that same scraping and
repainting of my old spiritual exterior, some setting down of
deeper roots in faith. I decided that I needed to devote a full
year to studying the Bible and to reading it from cover to
cover again. That resolution was to be fueled by a family
crisis that would stretch my Christian faith to its limits and
lead to a spiritual rebirth in my life.

At about this time a very dear friend in Calhoun became
seriously ill and we both felt the need for a circle of prayer
and study. I got together a dozen women from our town,
and we planned to read all the books of the Bible and to have
weekly study sessions at our house in Calhoun. We were still
commuting between Atlanta and Calhoun.

All my life I've been reading the Bible and step by step
and year by year I've learned more. As a child I liked the Old
Testament stories best—because they were *stories*, full of
character, action, plot, and passions—holy and not so holy. I
remember the Sunday school books with pictures of Joseph
in his striped coat of many colors. Another of him sad and
frightened, staring up out of a pit, and later in royal robes
standing on a dais judging and forgiving the brothers who
had wronged him. I was always puzzled and somewhat
afraid of struggling with an angel at night in my own room as
Jacob did on the banks of the brook Jabbok. The Old Testament stories communicated something of vast human complexity to me. I saw the vanity, pride and passion, but also
the faith, hope and obedience of these very human characters. It taught me about the worst and the best in people—it
was like a course in human nature, it prepared me for life.

In my middle years I turned to the Psalms. Those songs
of praise and cries for help, first uttered three thousand
years ago, seemed to give perfect expression to my fluctuat-
ing moments of joy and hours of deepest woe. They comforted me.

I knew all the books of the New Testament, but its profound depths were still not fully open to me. I wanted to try

to open myself up to them in a deeper way, this year especially. Step by step I had drawn closer to Jesus—now God required a year of discipline from me, a year devoted to his Word. I knew Jesus to this degree: in every obligation a gift is hidden. In every service we render there lies a reward. When we lift his yoke, we remove our own, and we discover his is light. So I looked forward with some anticipation to this year, because I felt the Lord was requiring it for a reason. He knew my weaknesses and my needs, and I felt sure he was preparing me for something unique, something new, something unparalleled before in my life.

Our study group met every Monday morning at 10:30. We started in July, 1975, and ended in July a year later.

At times there in Calhoun, there were as many as twelve or thirteen people who came to the Bible Study, and sometimes as few as two or three, but a strong core group was soon established. Our usual pattern was to begin and end with prayer, read a passage from the book we were studying that week, and then discuss it together. We usually shared insights for an hour and a half. It was marvelous to discover the wide range of reactions from these different women. The Lord speaks to us where we are, in so many different ways. Verses that I would read right over would have a special meaning for someone else. Some women were knowledgeable scholars of the Bible, others like me were well acquainted with it but still beginners at discovering its historical, theological and spiritual depths. I was especially grateful to our pastor's wife, Elise Brackman, for her insights into so many passages.

I now think of the events of that year in relationship to books of the Bible. During Christmas week we were reading Isaiah. To that point I had focused on and rejoiced in the prophecy of Christ's advent in Isaiah 7, 11 and 53. I associated Isaiah with Handel's *Messiah*. It was one of the books of the Old Testament I knew mostly from Christmas readings. But that year it brought me another message, a message of hope that I had not counted on. It sustained me through personal crisis.

Holiday times are hard on families. Joy is sometimes

diminished by the hustle and bustle; worship is sometimes overshadowed by commercialism. Recollections of times past and loved ones lost sometimes bring sadness. Pressures build up at work and home as people race to keep on schedule with shopping, entertaining and business deadlines.

Tram and Patty were living with us at Butterfly Manna. The first few years of marriage are always a time of adjustment, and their first few years were no exception. Just before Christmas when the pressures were great on all of us and extra heavy on Tram and Patty angry words caused some unresolved problems to surface. Perhaps some of the problems were caused by too much closeness, living as we all were under one roof. There was an almost complete breakdown of communication among us.

It was a fractious, anxious, tear-stained time for all of us, and as a result, we all spent a troubled, unsettled holiday. We took private consolation in the birth of our Savior, but were not able to deeply feel the joy among us that Christ brought to the world. I am thankful to God, however, that he repairs as well as creates. How often churches have failed to bring forth joy and fellowship, but they still exist by God's supporting grace. How many times have I, as an individual, failed to demonstrate love, forgiveness and forbearance? God forgives me and repairs the harm I've done. He held out the same promise to Tram and Patty. After a time their situation began to improve, but my mood seemed to continue to be dark. All my life some people have considered me lucky or pampered or blessed or just plain rich. They think such people never feel pain. And I've considered myself unusually blessed by God with more important "riches"— with family, friends, fellowship.

But here it was, Christmas, 1975, and I was living in a mansion in Atlanta, feeling my heart slowly break for my eldest son and my daughter-in-law. I felt guilty and depressed. What had I done wrong? How had I failed to teach and prepare them for life? I wondered what I could do to help. I wondered what I could have done. I looked back over the frantic changes that had been happening in our lives for the last four years, ever since Bert went to the Highway Department. Life had uprooted us; it had taken us from our children; it had cost us dearly in terms of self-sacrifice. Was that what God wanted? It had seemed so. Then why the problems? What was to be done about Tram and   ? God had cut out another human puzzle. How were we going to get the pieces into the shape and wholeness he had designed?

Bert and I talked to them. I think young people need to be assured that what they are experiencing is not unique. I knew this from my own marriage—they should have been able to see it in the marriages of other young people. Young people have such high expectations for marriage today. Far too many see it primarily in a romantic light as the union which legitimizes love and sex. Far too few see it as a social and religious unit, a partnership that demands work. A marriage is the union in which the work of life goes on; it is the basic unit of worship and fellowship—or should be. But young people today frequently come to marriage ill equipped, lacking the skills and the willingness they need to shoulder responsibility. Many are married directly out of school, or college, so they have never had to support themselves or anyone else. They have had most things done and arranged for them—everything from organized sports to buying their clothes.

Christian marriage is far more than a commitment to stay married just "because the Bible says so." It is the outward sign of two people's love endorsed in the name of Jesus. It is Christ who is the initial gatherer. He is the bridegroom of the church. It is he who sets his seal upon a marriage, and he who is the cohesive force of love. Marriage is a celebration and witness to the Lord who has chosen these two for each other out of the many thousands of possible mates. A marriage is made for prayer—marriage is a prayer, a living prayer which demonstrates the power of love over loneliness and unity over separateness.

Bert and I talked to the children, sharing our concern for them and confessing our own failures and doubts. Our marriage is a strong, working marriage. Our children know what that means. It does not mean that we've never had a day of trouble, pain or resentment. Carefree days such as that are reserved for heaven. On this earth conflict is our lot, but Christ is our hope. I have a quick and ugly tongue, which has caused me and others, Bert certainly, no end of trouble. I am fast to anger, slower to forgive or apologize. But Christ has given us time. A marriage is built on the long term. It's like buying or building a house. You take out a long-term policy, and you pay into it month after month until the house is finally all yours. I may be mean or angry or frustrated at one moment; nonetheless, I expect to prove my love over the next week, month, year, lifetime. And I work at marriage one day at a time.

That Christmas was a hard one, but it was a time of healing as well. I found myself in a most curious emotional state—up one minute, down the next. My moods were precarious, tense and tender. Once when I was decorating the front door of Butterfly Manna with a large wreath I broke out crying for no reason at all and had to run indoors. Christmas dinner was quite a strain. Fifty or so relatives and friends had arrived. There was laughter and gaiety, and I was laughing and carrying on myself, but I kept wondering "what's happening?" Is this me laughing, singing? I felt outside myself—close to bereavement. I felt as if I were mourning.

After the holidays things did not get better. The early days of January were bleak and rainy. I had a vision of the whole year stretching out interminably—and to what purpose? My life felt as if it were closing down. If I dressed nicely to go out, I'd look in the mirror and feel ugly. I had no confidence in my dress or appearance. If I stayed home I was bored and restless. And I wandered through room after room in Butterfly Manna looking for the right angle of sunlight, or some comforting niche to sit in and read, but nothing seemed to satisfy me.

I felt like a poor little rich girl. Here I was with sixty rooms and no place to sit, not one room I felt comfortable in. It was a startling realization, because I knew I had been fortunate. It proved, I suppose, that *things* do not make for genuine happiness. Good times, bad times, we all have them. But on the whole God has treated me gently. He has never over-strained my capacity to endure. Moreover, he has treated me gently in the spirit. Some people are racked by spiritual pain, doubt and spiritual vacillation, but I had grown easily, stage by stage, from Christian childhood toward a more mature faith. I had never been brought low. My strong self-image had rarely been challenged by adversity that had truly tested it. I had grown from strength, not weakness—yet here I had reached a point beyond which ego strength could not carry me. I could not with any power of my own change my mood, break my depression, toss off the feeling of guilt.

Up in the top story of the house, high in the attic among the large beamed rafters, Barker and I had made a small chapel. We decorated it with simple things—the kind of tapestries of the Last Supper you can buy at roadside stands in Georgia, old oak prayer benches, big brass candle-sticks, and two big dark pews from the old Calhoun Baptist Church. And though it's certainly not an elegant cathedral—it's warm; it's comfortable. It is a good private place for prayer and reflection. I don't normally go there every day, but just knowing it's there helps me. And usually when I have gone there to pray over a problem, I have found quiet and peace. But when I went there that lonely Christmas season I felt like a single candle burning in a dark hall. I felt isolated and alone.

Usually dark moods pass. All moods do, I assured my-self. But this one was persistent. I expected a change by the New Year. But nothing changed. I plummeted into a period of depression—one of those conditions where you spiral down and down. "Is this despair?" I asked myself. What reason do I have for despair? Tram and Patty were having problems but were beginning to patch things up. I had every reason to be happy. As I looked back over the past four years I realized that we had had as many successes as we had had defeats. We were richer, more prominent, had greater influ-ence and a better opportunity to witness for our Lord than before. Why wasn't I happy? What was wrong with me?

My mood began to turn in on me. I went from a preoccu-pation with events, things and people around me to consid-

erations of the fundamental character defects that have always plagued me. Why did I strike out at people? Why did I
try to have things my own way? Why was I always so
finicky? Why couldn't I control my temper? Why? And from
those and other thoughts I convinced myself that I was
totally unlovable. Curiously, rather than trying to make myself more pleasing and agreeable to others, I became the very
thing I feared. I became more snippy, moody, hard to please.
Like the apostle Paul, I did the very things I did not want to
do. I cried easily. Left the room often. Food had no taste, salt
no savor. Bert must have been at his wit's end with me. I
certainly was in no shape to entertain his friends. And I
certainly wasn't helping my family.

Bert and I went out to a party on the evening of January 1,
and while we were driving to our friend's house Bert tried to
comfort me.

"Darling, you've got to get hold of yourself. You can't
blame yourself for everything." He appeared rather somber
himself.

"I can't help it," I said. "I just can't help myself out of
this."

"Well, nobody can. Some things you can control, others
you can't. This is one you can't. 'So let go and let God,' as the
pastor said last Sunday. Turn it over to the Lord and let that
be that."

But I couldn't. I felt myself gripping the front door handle
of the car so hard my fingers had turned numb. I felt as if I
were losing control. If I could have opened that door,
jumped out and run away, I would have. But how do you
run away from yourself? How do you keep the top spinning
upright when it's beginning to tilt dangerously askew. The
shadows of trees and the glare of lights washing up and over
the front window looked threatening and foreboding.

Later I tried to write. On January 8, 1976, I started to keep
a journal. I kept a note pad by my bed in case something
would occur to me during the night. I felt a great need to
describe and define my feelings, and to put my frustrations
and longings down on paper. These words came out mostly
in rhyme, and I suppose the best term for them would be

simply "yearnings" of my soul. I would also take my journal out into the courtyard when the day began to warm, and sit on a stone bench, listen to the fountain and write. And since we began to travel quite a lot in January of that year I learned to write in any place where a thought struck me—airports, hotels, taxis. The words poured out—and I felt they came from God.

I can now follow the cycle of my spirit day after day in my journal. It is a sort of *Pilgrim's Progress*—written with swift certainty. I can see the day-by-day renewal of my spiritual strength. But I had to begin at the bottom—where a reduced and humbled soul cries out—oh how miserable I am. I am nothing. I am sinful. I dread myself and my fate. Help me, Lord! I need you. And at that point, strength broken, I sensed arms bearing me up; hopeless, I found hope; dead to myself, I found new life. Where formerly I thought I knew God the Father, now I committed my new life to God the Son, and I felt born again.

I went to bed on January 7 in a tumult of feelings—rage, despair, self-hatred, helplessness—and awoke, after a dream, full of sensation—I was filled with awe, fear and yet the peace to write this poem which begins my spiritual journey and my journal. I heard God say, "Write," and I promised I would write whatever he gave me for one year.

January 8, 1976
What is this thing called Life
Whereupon we meet with strife
Where our days are so numbered
With so many burdens encumbered—
Where it is always a debate for the right—
Oh God, preserve me
Pray endure me
To rise among ashes
To your freedom and light.

Long ago I had been stirred to my first real encounter with God by the parable of the workers in the vineyard. I see it now as a parable of my own life. I see a long, long field of cotton at morning time. The mist is still rising off the ground and the shadowy shapes of the laborers are gathering in the dim light, taking up their sacks, and setting out in staggering lines through the boll-bursting fields. All day long they come, wave after wave, because the field is huge. The hardy workers come, the weak ones, derelicts who need a buck, children on a lark, desperate ones just trying to make a living. They come all day and at the setting sun, the strong and weak, the gristled grandfather and the little child bring in their sacks. Two strong hands lift the load from them. One by one they are raised to the scales and the weighing arm swings in a mighty arc across the gulf of eternity. All who have come—early or late—are paid the premium price, all receive a substantial reward. All get what they do not deserve. This is grace. God's free gift to sinfun man.

This simple poem was for me a birth announcement—a sign of my awakening from an earthly sleep to a new awareness of Jesus Christ. I won my struggle with myself by surrender. I raised the white flag over my embattled ego and let God take over the armistice and reconstruction.

I was one of the late workers to enter the vineyard. All my life I had been working around the periphery, you might say. I was tending the ditches that brought in water; I was marketing the grapes; I was coordinating the shipment and transportation of workers and produce. But I had not fully resigned myself, emptied myself to get right down to the selfless toil in the vineyard itself. Finally I came. And I praise God that he cares not whether it is late or soon. Come and cry out to him and believe in him and hold onto him and receive the glory and eternal life through his son Jesus Christ. "Behold, I stand at the door and knock. . . ." Open the door, and be free of the enclosure of self. Crack open the shell of ego and let God rule your will.

I think of ego and sin and Christ's all-forgiving love in this little formula: Ego is the "I" in *sin*. If you remove the "i" and replace it with the "o" from *love* you get *Son*—Jesus, God's Son, who is sent to free us from sin by love. I can date my rebirth January 8, 1976, but that's not important. There's too much said about "birthdays." The date, the place, the condition, the trial, the sins and washing away of sins smacks too much, to my way of thinking, of praying aloud in the Temple. I try to shy away from pious words that are empty. What is important is that one *is* God's, not how one *becomes* God's, that the Son is at the center of one's life, not sin. What is important is that one is in the vineyard working.

From then on my burdens began to lighten. I did not expect God to completely heal everything overnight—not my self-wounded heart or our family problems—but God had lanced the infection and started the healing. And the progress was sure and steady.

I kept writing and the words of my poems just seemed to pour out as a gift, a revelation from God. Poems and praise came by the pageful until I started to measure the output in reams, inches of paper sheets.

Perhaps 1976 would not be such a bad year after all, I thought. Little did I then suspect that it would be a year that would change our lives again in a most dramatic way. Change would once again come through a friend we had come to know and love. But in January of 1976 he was still a fairly unknown figure or an enigma to most Americans. Few considered him a serious presidential candidate. A man named Jimmy Carter was still stumping on the political trail from New Hampshire's cold to Florida's balmy beaches.

I continued writing poetry. It became an extremely important spiritual exercise—the fulfillment of a promise to write what God would direct every day for a year. I had never written much before, perhaps an occasional verse for a birthday or a Christmas poem for Bert; but then out of prayer and this personal crisis, I started writing prolifically. The words fairly flowed out of me. I wrote every day for over a year, wrote as fast as my hand could move in some cases. It seemed that God was communicating both to me and through me. Many of the poems dealt with Bible interpretation. I collected some short ones together and put one long poem in booklet form. Bert was amazed and pleased at this production and suggested that I have a secretary to type them up and help organize them.

God led me to write poems on different sections of the

Bible and paramount Bible themes. *Praises to the Lord* is a collection of poems that take themes similar to Psalms. *Prophecies from God* deals with the interpretation of the Book of Revelation, putting Bible prophecy in relation to events happening today, which impress me as being signs of the latter days. I also wrote many shorter poems on contemporary concerns, poems that show how Christ can make an impact on a person's life today. These poems address people where they are and make a strong call for a turn to God. I call them *Strength for these Days*.

A Story from God is a narrative poem which Bert and I had published in a small booklet of fifty pages to give to friends. It takes the main stories and points of the Bible chronologically and book by book, underscoring God's plan of salvation. It puts this plan in easily readable, greatly condensed form. I believe this little book can be used as an introduction to the Bible by both children and adults who aren't familiar with it or want to be reacquainted with Scripture. I have given away hundreds of copies of this little book to friends, congressmen, cabinet officers, world leaders, and it seems to have touched a responsive chord in many hearts.

A Story from God was written while Bert and I were at the Democratic Convention in New York City in the summer of 1976. We were not delegates, but many of Jimmy Carter's friends from Georgia were there. It was a glorious and exciting time, and I think the feeling that I was in the middle of a place and situation where history was being made may have contributed to the inspiration I felt in writing about the immense historical sweep of the Bible. Just think how the Bible has affected lives throughout the centuries. It shows the action of God over a span of six thousand years of human history in his attempts to draw man to him. If there was any perspective America needed in 1976—and at any time—it was that of God's hand is on human affairs.

Bert and I had been to New York many times before—with the boys on vacation and on business trips—but I never failed to be moved by this place. New York is a living symbol of America and the dreams of the masses. If one central image of our heritage is the democratic forum of the village of free men and equals, the other is of the great melting pot—the city as the place of generating economic life and promise. New York with all its problems still stirred me in this way. Whether I was shopping on Fifth Avenue or mingling with the crowds at the convention, I felt the pulse of the city. It fairly hummed like a huge generator of ideas, business, people's hopes and aspirations.

Then on the final night of the convention we heard Jimmy give his acceptance speech. We sat with the Carter family. I was proud, hearing his declaration of pride and hope for America, hearing him speak of his love for this country and his love of his family and his God. Surely, I thought, God is acting again, bringing some new ray of his grace to our land. A Christian President may or may not be a better President politically—but he will at least do one thing that is absolutely vital for our nation and the world at this time: call on God and work toward his glory through repentance and peace.

I have always believed in Jimmy Carter, and I do not claim to be prophetic, but in this case the polls and I agreed. I believed he would win the Presidency, and become a great President as well. The mere fact that he would be the first President from the South in one hundred years had to be significant. That alone would do something positive for this nation where regionalism and division are still to some extent a fact, and where prejudice and false images often rule. Jimmy Carter's election would be a symbolic realization of the New South, of the industrial progress and economic growth and good government for which both Jimmy and Bert had worked—a symbol of national unity.

Neither Bert nor I had played a prominent role in Jimmy's campaign. Bert had introduced him to some bankers and business leaders and had spoken for him on numerous occasions, but that was about the extent of his involvement. Bert was very much absorbed in the promotional and administrative functions of the National Bank of Georgia. He loved banking and it was gratifying to him that he was achieving the goals he had set for himself and fulfilling the hopes the board of directors had of him when they hired him. He was brought into the business to help the bank grow. So it was pleasing that in the two years he had served as President of NBG, total assets had nearly doubled. And the loan business of the bank had greatly increased. All this being the case, Bert had no notion or particular desire to serve in the federal government.

After the election he was surprised to get a call from President-elect Carter asking if he would be willing to join the Administration. How would he leave his post at the bank? How would it affect our family and finances? What would be his task? All these questions and many more ran through his mind.

It's our custom to hold family meetings every day around the dining table when important matters arise in our family. Everyone gets a chance to talk and to listen to the others. We try to reach an agreement, with Bert's view usually prevailing if the problem calls for a single action on the part of the entire family. When Bert came home with news of Jimmy's invitation to join the Cabinet, it was like a bolt out of the blue. It would change so much. We all needed to discuss it. We were at home in Atlanta.

"It's a great honor, Daddy," David said. He was proud, but cautious.

"But is it what you want?" I asked. Frankly I was happy with the life we had. It had taken time to work out suitable arrangements with our family living in Atlanta and Calhoun.

"I'm not yet sure myself. But it's hard to turn down a direct request from the President," Bert said.

"I'm not going to Washington. I don't want to—I want to stay with my friends in Calhoun," Beverly said. "I'm not moving. No way!"

At age fifteen, I knew he needed stability and the security of home, family and friends. I knew how the boys' lives had been interrupted and altered by our campaigning and our move to Atlanta. I knew that Beverly was really happy in Calhoun.

"Whatever we do, we should try to decide as a family," I said. "We need to work out a solution that each of us can live with."

"Well, Tram's off on his own now and I'll be starting college soon so it doesn't affect us as much," Stuart said.

All the boys had had to bear a share of the load of our public life. For them it had meant seeing less of us, having to fend for themselves in some cases, growing up too fast. The shadows cast over them from the limelight falling on Bert were not always pleasant. Teenagers want to be part of the group and our public life had set them apart. Reporters went digging into their private lives as well as Bert's and mine.

"It's such a big step, Bert. Can we afford to take another big step? It seems as if we have been gypsies these last few years," I said.

"That's true. And it would mean a dramatic cut in salary," Bert said. "But it's a matter of duty. A citizen owes something to his country. I can't turn my back on a nation that's given us so much. In a free society we all must pay the 'rent.'"

We discussed the matter from every angle, but it became clear that Bert felt it was a responsibility he could not refuse. And already I could sense his warming to the challenge. He was a man who had never retreated from challenge. Bert had started with little and had been given much. Of him much was expected. He believed that verse. He had built one small bank into a financial center for a whole district and the whole new burgeoning carpet industry. He had taken another fine old Georgia banking institution and given it a new shot of adrenalin, and it was growing. And now he was offered the opportunity to try to do the same thing for America, to confront the economic problems of energy, recession, pollution, employment and so many other pressing problems of the mid-70s. He had a chance to be part of the team that would lead the United States into its third century. He could help inject a stimulus that would carry the country forward. How could a man such as he refuse? We would work out the difficulties, rearrange our lives, find a way for the two young boys to finish their education in Calhoun and Atlanta, and get back on the road ourselves once again. It was expected of us. It was the right thing to do.

At that point we didn't know what the post would be, but we decided that it must be something to do with banking, the treasury, or commerce. So I was surprised when Bert told me a day later, after he had talked with Jimmy, that it was the Office of Management and Budget. I wasn't thoroughly clear what the head of that office did. Bert explained that it was a post that budgeted and reviewed the financial operations of all federal agencies. The job seemed to be a tremendous one. Jimmy Carter had valued Bert's performance in government and his ability to push through legislation, especially dealing with the reorganization of Georgia state departments. Now he was calling on Bert to initiate the same restructuring of federal agencies from the position of Director of OMB. It was just the sort of challenge that Bert loves. He couldn't say no.

Washington

Washington! The White House! Bert serving in the Cabinet of the United States of America! I had to pause for a moment and draw a breath. What wonders the Lord performs. A few years ago we were quietly bringing up our family in a small north Georgia town, happy, content, attempting to do our part for our community and church, and then all of a sudden this widening expanding circle of political involvement, a whole new course for us, an entirely new realm of service. Who else but God could have done it! It was not something we had sought. And in Washington, what new things had God to reveal to us, and through us? We waited upon his time and will.

In December Bert took a plane down to Plains to meet with Jimmy Carter, Fritz Mondale, Cyrus Vance and several others for a strategy session. Arriving early and not finding anyone at the airfield to pick him up, he borrowed someone's old pickup and drove himself to the meeting. Newsmen were waiting outside the President-elect's farm and Bert made quite a stir driving up in the old farm vehicle. "This is a Carter limousine," he declared. "Boy, are things going to be different when we get to Washington!" It was typical of Bert's light and easy manner with the press. He clearly enjoyed them, and he knew that the press had a job to do. He tried to accommodate them. They seemed to like Bert. He was good copy because he was friendly, expansive, open to all of them, never evasive.

Even after our stint on the governor's campaign trail I was surprised by the press, however. There were so many reporters around the President, constantly. And it is surprising the things they deemed newsworthy. The media consume words, print, images, information. Something "new" has to be said, shown or printed every day and every night, even when there is not much news to report. Every gesture of the President and his circle is viewed, reviewed, analyzed, interpreted. Their choice of words, their moods, their families, their habits, tastes, even their clothes will be commented upon. When Bert leased a car for our family during the inauguration days, the company put his name on the license plate. They were proud to be driving our family, I guess, but it made the national press. When the President-elect and his advisers met for an initial series of meetings at his farm and at Sea Island and dressed casually, it was noted in the press as being an indicator of a new era of openness and informality in government. The press was there in droves wherever the President went. When he came to our Sea Island place and he and Bert planned to go swimming, the press covered the beach. Later when the President and Amy came to our house for a casual dinner while Rosalynn was on a trip, the press covered it almost like a full state occasion.

There was tremendous excitement in the air those early days and finally the boys and I began to catch it. Just think—being able to play a part in the growth of good government, restoring public confidence in the Presidency, setting the country on a new course.

Bert also told me that President Carter wanted to involve the wives and families in his administration. He did not want to cut his men off from their homes and from the people, isolating them in a siege tower of politics as had been so common in previous administrations. Concern for families and the moral fabric of the nation was to be his watchword.

This was reflected in Jimmy's acceptance speech as the Democratic Party's presidential candidate, which dealt with the need to strengthen family life. Walter Mondale was the Senate's staunchest defender of children. Joseph Califano, who became Secretary of Health, Education and Welfare, had been Jimmy's campaign adviser on the family. I believed in the vital importance of this issue too, and was glad that it would be practiced as well as preached by the President's staff.

Wives would be briefed about all but top secret matters concerning their husbands' work, we were all promised. Rosalynn asked the Cabinet wives to play a role helping as hostesses at the White House and in other activities. The President frequently held Cabinet briefing sessions which spouses would attend. In fact, both Bert and I got a crash-course in the federal government, learning how the Office of Management and Budget related to all other federal agencies. I read many reports, briefs and position papers that came to Bert.

When Bert agreed to join the Cabinet, we had to put all our financial holdings in a blind trust. This was to insure that there would be no conflict of interest while he was in government service. President Carter's guidelines in this regard were made public and quite strict. We had to set up the trust quickly because transition time was short and Bert, as the first Cabinet appointee, was expected to be in the thick of organizing the new administration. Bert's particular position required immediate action. He had to get a grasp on the budget prepared by the Ford Administration before Congress met, because he would be responsible for presenting the budget changes that the Carter Administration wanted. In short, we quickly had to put our financial affairs in the hands of others, and the rush—necessary as it was—cost us dearly. Later, guidelines on finances were made less strict.

When Bert agreed to sell 200,000 shares of the National Bank of Georgia stock before the end of the year, the natural thing happened. The public annoucement of his intention to sell such a large block of stock immediately sent the price of the shares on a downward trend. People who know the stock market know that when there are more shares for sale than there are immediate buyers, the price of the stock drops. And that's what happened. If we could have kept it secret that we were going to sell the stock, and put it on the market a little at a time, this might not have happened. But when you make a promise at a hearing in the United

States Senate, there's no chance for secrecy. This drop in the value of the stock was to greatly affect our political fortune later. It was when Bert sought to delay selling the stock in early summer, because it had fallen in value and we stood to lose a good deal of money, that the press began to speculate on our financial situation, creating the impression that Bert was a near-bankrupt wheeler-dealer. But Bert owed it to the thousands of owners of NBG stock not to sell off all his stock while it was in a downward spiral—that would have depressed the stock even further and caused undue damage to the life savings of others. We could cover our loses if we had to, but what of others?

That first month, December of 1976, we were living out of suitcases in hotels. Bert was busy with the transition at OMB and I started looking for a permanent place to live. I didn't know Washington at all, but I soon found that Georgetown with its picturesque streets and old townhouses was just what I was looking for. And I quickly found the perfect place —a three-story red brick townhouse, available for lease—a rare find in Washington. I loved it, and it was convenient for Bert, just ten minutes or so from his office.

My brother Barker helped me again to get furniture up from Atlanta and Calhoun. We put a gold federal eagle on the door. The owner was so kind. She helped me select colors and had the interior painted. We were lucky to get some painters in over Christmas. So the house was ready by the first of the year. I had most of the downstairs rooms done in pleasing light blues and yellows, and I reworked the drapes left in the house and added others—yellow organdy in the kitchen. I put in pale blue carpets that had been made in Georgia.

During our first months in Washington, Bert and I took long walks in the evening down Georgetown's streets, along the dark slow waters of the Potomac, near the Jefferson Memorial and around the Mall. The lights played on the famous buildings and monuments, turning the city into a huge, glittering machine. But as the noise of traffic faded and the streets and paths grew quiet, an older habit of mind returned to me—the Southern girl in me was listening and looking. Barn owls that nest in the roofs of the Smithsonian were on the wing, the screech of bats and nighthawks filled the vast dome of night over the empty and silent Mall. Here I sensed history, felt our national heritage coming alive with this living city where there was love and laughter, people, parties, politics, the pulse of a nation beating in the hearts of her people.

We were thrilled by Washington. And tried to be open with its people and reporters. The newspapers and *Time* and *Newsweek* sent people to interview us. Everybody was interested in what the "New Government People" were like; everyone was wondering who would be the new movers and shakers in this town built on power, personalities and politics. What would be the new style? It is amazing how people tend to misread other people. I read that I was "fragile," "tough," "sweet," "cold," "a camellia from the Old South," and that I was expected to be the new "social lioness" of Washington. Amazing! No matter how many times I told reporters that I saw myself as a wife and mother first and foremost, they seemed to want or expect me to be something or someone else.

Mistakes happened easily and often, even with simple facts. Butterfly Manna was variously reported as a 40, 50, or 60-room house. When *Time* printed a photo of our George-town house it was the wrong house—I'd never seen it before.

Most of the reporters had good intentions. But we weren't exempt from the controversial. In early January *The Washington Post* picked up information that was old news in Georgia about Bert's gubernatorial campaign financing, our financial position and the Calhoun bank management.

On January 8 *The Washington Post* carried a story with the headline: "U.S. Probed Lance Campaign: Found No Ground to Prosecute." This article mentioned the Justice Department's thorough investigation of the campaign financing and overdrafts at the Calhoun Bank (which was basically a matter of transfers from one account to another).

On January 11 *The New York Times* printed an article entitled: "U.S. Investigation of Lance Closed Day Before Carter Appointed Him." A third story appeared on January

16, again in *The Times*, which discussed banking practices at the Calhoun bank and overdrafts concerning the gubernatorial campaign.

All these news stories appeared before the Senate confirmation hearings began on January 17. So by that early date all the essentials of the "Lance Affair," as it was called later in the year, were known to the press, the Senate and the people. Why and how did the atmosphere which lead to Bert's approval by the Senate in January change to what Haynes Johnson, a writer for *The Washington Post*, on the morning of Bert's resignation, September 22, called a "vendetta atmosphere"?

In his column entitled, "On Lance: What Did the Media Know and When?" he said, "Even some members of the press are speaking of a 'vendetta' atmosphere present among the correspondents and news organizations. The press is either out to 'get' Carter and his Georgians by 'getting' Lance, or is trying to 'get' news rivals who may have triumphed in earlier competitive contests."

It was ironic that these early stories contained the substance of all the information and accusations that were to be repeated and repeated and analyzed and reanalyzed as "news" in July, August and September. But in those early euphoric first days of the Carter Presidency, the press was more tolerant, there was other important news and we were happy to have made a thorough disclosure of our personal and financial history to government investigative bodies and to the public.

President Carter had set high ethical standards for his administration. We believed by Bert's making a full disclosure of his private and business dealings we were keeping both the letter and the spirit of these standards. Anyone who has ever run a business or worked in a political campaign knows that there may be overdrafts or other problems. We did not claim that we had never had problems or had made no mistakes, only that we had made full restitution and that we had shown everything that had transpired in our past and trusted that our intentions and character would be seen to have been consistently honorable and ethical. We were trying to do what was right. Any and all overdrafts had been paid. And both the Calhoun Bank and the National Bank of Georgia, far from suffering under Bert's management, had grown and grown. The NBG assets had in fact doubled; the Calhoun Bank had assets of about six million when Bert took over—and over sixty million when he went to Washington. It was the largest bank for its population base of any bank in the country.

On January 17 and 18 the Senate Governmental Affairs Committee convened to hold confirmation hearings on Bert. All the governmental agency reports were presented, including the FBI's and Comptroller of the Currency's office reports and Bert's own financial statement listing our assets and liabilities. The committee recommended Bert's confirmation on the 18th, the whole Senate approved it two days later. The Cabinet Officers were sworn in by Chief Justice Warren Burger in the East Room of the White House on January 23, 1977. I held the Bible for Bert that the boys had bought for the occasion.

It was a day I'll always remember with pride. Our family was there, Barker and his wife, Rita, Bert's sister, Alice Rose, and her husband, Frank McAfee, my mother and stepfather, Ronald Chance. Our Christian brother and sister, the Carters, received Bert into the honored task of helping guide this great nation. It is a memory I cherish—which subsequent events made more poignant but cannot erase.

Bert plunged immediately into the important tasks before him. Not only was he responsible for the budget, but it was soon apparent that the President wanted him to be the Administration's ambassador to industry and businessmen. The President also discussed and sometimes sought his advice about tax rebates, departmental expenditures, zero-based budgeting, legislation, governmental appointments, and other issues.

The early period of news coverage was most concerned with the personalities of the Carter team and the political direction that the Administration would be taking. When the Senate met in January it found neither the news stories nor the special reports by the FBI and other agencies to contain anything so problematical as to call Bert's appointment into question. In time the political climate

changed to the point where the very same facts and reports
became the source for "evidence" regarding Bert's case.
New headlines, same stories. It almost seemed that the more
Bert's influence and closeness with the President became
known, the more he was singled out for attack.

One of the early controversies of the Carter Presidency
concerned the B-1 Bomber. President Carter's stand for
strong national defense and his naval engineer's demand for
detailed military cost accounting are well known. It was his
decision that this costly arms project, which did not improve
our defense posture, be eliminated. It was a courageous
action—one of the few times in recent decades that a sitting
President had turned down a major military construction
program. Bert was one of the Cabinet officers who believed
that the B-1 project was economically and militarily ques-
tionable. The military and armament lobbies in Congress are
the most powerful of all. And the President and Bert both
had to take a drubbing. It seemed too that zero-based
budgeting and governmental restructuring was viewed with
alarm within the agencies. Every administration has a hard
row to hoe in establishing its priorities. Opposition, we
knew, was at the heart of political life, and we were not afraid
of it. But we were to learn how personal that opposition can
become.

I, of course, was not on this firing line, but every wife
feels and fights her husband's battles even more keenly than
her own. Fortunately, I was encircled by new friends and
prayer partners. Shortly after we got settled in Georgetown,
I invited Cabinet wives to join me in a prayer group which
met at our house. We met every Tuesday morning, visited,
had coffee and tea and prayed about the national issues that
our husbands faced at work. We prayed that they would
make the right decisions and follow the path God has set for
this country.

I was also teaching a Bible class for senior citizens at the
Dumbarton Avenue Methodist Church, right down the
street from our townhouse. This was a real blessing to me
because many of these older people loved their Bible and
really knew it. They had insights into Scripture that constantly illuminated and deepened my reading. We read Rev-

elation, Jonah, James, and the Psalms. They had an attitude about life and the pace of life that would be a good corrective for the ego and the go-go pressures of official Washington. I developed a close relationship with the whole group. These lovely people helped me through the most difficult days.

The greatest joy of this period, indeed of the whole year, was the birth of our first grandson, Thomas Bertram Lance III, in April, 1977. Tram and Patty were beaming parents—their happiness seemed complete. A seal had been set upon their marriage which held them more closely together. Bert was the typical grandfather—at moments shy and then beaming with pride as he bounced his new grandson on his knee. I felt the gentle movement of the generations. All the love, joy, sorrow, pain that I had known would be his—this newborn child's. God is good. He gives us life and whirls the crystal clock of creation. He fills the earth with abundant love. Little "Trey" was our best diversion from political troubles.

On May 23rd *Time* magazine reported details of our loan from the First National Bank of Chicago which refinanced an earlier loan from a New York bank. At each stage of these public announcements very little new information was offered, but the political pressure increased. Nothing was stated categorically, but it was implied that influence peddling and other shady business dealings were involved. I was not worried at this point, for everyone assured me that this was just the typical kind of heat that came with working in the political kitchen. If you were in politics, they said, you were going to get some criticism. I already knew that, and so I wasn't disturbed. I knew my husband—that, for me, was enough. I knew Bert would never do anything illegal. I rested on the truth. Many papers were critical of the way he handled business at the Calhoun bank—but they did not know Calhoun or how depressed northern Georgia was until bankers and businessmen like Bert "energized" it by taking reasonable risks to build business and jobs. They did not know how many individual acts had helped people.

There was a month of breathless accusations and reports before the Senate Governmental Affairs Committee called Bert back on July 22, to clear the air about the allegations in the news. After thoroughly questioning Bert about our Chicago bank loan and other matters, the committee found that Bert had done nothing wrong, and Senator Ribicoff said that Bert had been smeared by the press. After the hearing, Bert and I both breathed a sigh of relief.

"Is it over now?" I asked.

"You can't be sure, but I hope so," he said. "It would be good to get the hearings over and get down to work. There's so much the President wants me to do. Some things aren't going to make me any more popular, I guess."

"What do you mean?" I asked.

"The President wants me to lead the effort to reorganize the federal agencies, just as we did in Georgia. People are afraid for their jobs. But we don't plan radical surgery, we just want to reorganize so there will be efficiency in all the departments. We'll reduce staff by attrition as people retire. There's going to be opposition, though."

"If it's a good goal, then you'll have to do it." I said. "And I know you'll do it so people inside the agencies and all the people outside are well served." But I detected something of a cloud over his spirits which was unusual for Bert. I guessed that there was going to be more about us in the news. I prayed that it would reflect facts and not political pressure.

Following the Senate's hearing, John G. Heimann, Comptroller of Currency, questioned Bert further about our loans. And later that day, August 5th, Bert held a press conference giving all the information regarding our loan from First National Bank of Chicago, detailing the collateral he put up for that loan which included our National Bank of Georgia stock and insurance policies. To make absolutely sure that the public was getting all the facts, the Comptroller ordered the Internal Revenue Service to determine if information regarding the loans or Bert's banking practices had been withheld from the FBI, which had investigated him and presented its report to the Senate confirmation hearings in January. On August 10th the Securities and Exchange Commission began inquiries into the National Bank of Georgia.

The pressure began to rise. On August 13th, before the Comptroller's report was in, Representative John B. Anderson, the third ranking Republican in the House, called for Bert's resignation.

What was happening? I began to wonder. Events seemed to be turning over and over the same facts, stories, rumors and as the media gazed longer and longer at these same facts and figures the mood began to darken.

The Cabinet wives were just great at this time. I got lots of encouragement and lots of prayer. And something else started to happen. All of a sudden letters of support and prayer letters, passages from Scripture and telegrams saying that people were lifting us up in prayer started arriving. You would expect letters from friends and acquaintances, but these were from unknown people across the country. All they knew about us was that we were Christians in government service—Christians who witnessed to that fact—and they wanted to express their love and support for what we represented.

My fourth grade teacher, Mrs. Lang, is one of Bert's mother's dearest friends, and very dear and special to me. We have corresponded regularly for years. She was very upset about our problems and her letters to me were filled with scriptural support. At the height of our troubles, she sent me in an envelope of dainty linen cutwork a lace handkerchief which she said I had given her as a gift on some occasion years and years ago. She had kept it carefully and returned it to me then as a token of her affection. Expressions of love such as these kept us afloat.

Helen Burns, wife of Arthur Burns, then Chairman of the Federal Reserve Board, who is himself a banker, was a good friend and a great comfort to me during this difficult time. We had lunch together two or three times while the various inquiries and hearings were going on. She must have known I needed someone to talk to during the days when Bert was being grilled and cross-examined. Helen was always perceptive. She knew that in some ways it was harder on the wife, who can't get angry, can't have her day in court, can't show a worried or crestfallen face in public. She had been in Washington a long time and knew how hard it could be at times. Not only were we both the wives of bankers, but Helen and I both wrote poetry. Rather than give

me advice which I couldn't heed, she simply showed calmness, kindness and concern. She was a truly good spirit-
booster during that time.

"The media are fickle," another Washington friend told
me. "You're on page one now only because these are the dog
days of summer and not much is happening in Washington.
Congress is in recess. If a real news story breaks you'll be
forgotten, and the committees can do their work in peace
without all the partisan pressure and media hype. You'll
survive."

I knew I'd survive. A bad reputation is not something
that worries Bert or me if we believe we are doing what is
right. Someone is not going to like you no matter what you
do. We learned that long ago. You only can do what you're
able and try to perceive what God wants—and then leave the
rest in his hands. Besides we are not "media" people. Our
lives would not sink or rise on what the media said about us.
The things that were important to us—each other, our family
and friends—could not be touched by a bad press. Often
when a reporter would interview me or Bert, they'd ask,
"How do you feel?" expecting us to say or show in some way
that we were being crushed by the grinding public attention.
But it just wasn't so. Neither of us was losing sleep. Our lives
went on because we trusted God that we would live in spite
of conflict—we had faced so many personal crises that mat-
tered more. Many people seem to believe today that truth
and reality are what they see on television, but what is real
and true is what happens in our homes and in our hearts. We
were not being crushed or strangled where our hearts
were—our consciences were clear.

On August 18th the Comptroller's report came in. It
termed some of the Calhoun banking practices unsound,
pointing particularly to the time period when Bert was at
at the Transportation Department and running for governor,
when he was not in charge on a day-to-day basis. But it
found no prosecutable offenses. So once again the same
ground had been gone over and no illegalities were found.
That day, after he had read the report, President Carter held
a news conference and affirmed his "complete confidence

and support" of his friend Bert Lance. He said, "Bert, I'm proud of you." I also read the report and it said, "no violations or illegalities."

It gratified us deeply that the President would say that about Bert and that he remained steadfastly loyal to Bert as a friend. Not *blindly* loyal, but steadfast, supportive in both prayer and in public. There was no question but that the pressure on Bert was construed by everyone to also be pressure on the President. Every news conference he held turned into a session on Bert. How long could the President stand it? Would he sacrifice his people at the first sign of conflict? Would the President be guided and his ranks divided by partisan politics and political pressure? In some ways Bert was a symbol, the front man for some the President's policies on governmental restructuring, zero-based budgeting and fiscally responsible military expenditure. How would the President then react to these pressures? The media could decide however they wanted, but we knew how good and strong the President was to us. He was fair, he was firm. He laid out the alternatives for Bert, but Bert knew that he himself was expected to make the ultimate decision regarding his political fate.

Through the rest of August more details on the management of the Calhoun bank, Bert's use of the bank's airplane, and reports of the various investigations, were made public. But on September 5th the mood took a darker turn; Senators Abraham A. Ribicoff and Charles H. Percy publically reported some wild allegations from a former Calhoun bank officer who was imprisoned for embezzling. I was heartsick. It seems Senators were running around like reporters saying things without substantiation or fact. They even publicly repeated the allegations of a convicted felon who was bargaining for a lighter sentence at the expense of my husband's reputation. It was Bert who had discovered the embezzlement and turned this man in. The embezzlement had long ago been investigated by the proper federal authorities, and the sole person responsible was brought to justice. Nothing to this day has ever shown that anyone in the Calhoun bank except the embezzler himself was engaged in any illegalities.

I was still opposed to buckling under to political pressure. I had expressed a strong opinion at a meeting held at Marshwinds on Sea Island over the Labor Day weekend.

Hamilton Jordan, the President's senior staffer, came down to meet with us on Saturday. He urged Bert to take a leave of absence from the OMB. That, he argued, would allow Bert time to settle his financial affairs and give the media the opportunity to find another target. Bert called Alex Smith, our Atlanta lawyer, and other close friends and sought their advice. Then Bert, Hamilton, Tram, David and I debated the idea long into the night. Finally we decided that Bert must have a chance to go before the Senate and the people to clear his name.

Hamilton returned to Washington on Sunday and briefed the President. We saw him on Monday, Labor Day afternoon. He agreed to the plan of Bert's going before the Senate committee again, before a final assessment regarding Bert's service in office would be made. He felt that things had been blown out of proportion, and he was pleased that Bert had chosen Clark Clifford to represent him.

I had argued for Bert to go before the Senate committee as soon as possible. What I didn't know was that the committee was going to postpone for a whole week Bert's chance to testify. I had expected Bert to be heard on the Thursday immediately after Labor Day.

Clark Clifford also was a factor in the decision to postpone Bert's appearance. He wanted time to get all the details straight in his own mind. Bert had never had a lawyer with him in any of his previous appearances, but we felt he ought to try it once the "Washington way," and have his attorney sitting beside him. Mr. Clifford is a well-known and highly repected figure in Washington, and that was also something to be considered. People on the Hill knew that if Clark Clifford took a case, it was a good case, and that the facts presented would be truthful and in full.

We also felt that if Bert were to take a leave of absence, it would be strategic to have Clark Clifford and his assistant, Robert Altman, in Washington to speak for Bert while we were in Georgia, in case other allegations were raised.

Since almost all the questions and documents raised in the course of the hearings dated back years, Alex Smith, who was a close friend of the family and the attorney for the National Bank of Georgia, was compiling old records for us.

The media meanwhile had still not found another target.

Another example is illustrative of the way in which data was distorted in that intensified atmosphere. The Washington press corps has been accustomed over the years to exposing senators and generals who ride on corporate jets, or military planes, or Cabinet officers who hire personal chefs and such at government expense. They were conditioned to react to "revelations" about Bert in these terms. But business use and custom regarding planes is quite different.

A Herblock cartoon showing Bert asked "Would you buy a used plane from this man?" calling attention to Bert's having paid $80,000 for the plane that he later sold to the National Bank of Georgia for $120,000.

But Bert had spent $33,000 on new engines for the plane, and redecorated the interior and made other repairs. And two years after Bert sold the bank the plane—after two years of additional use and depreciation—the bank was still able to sell it for $117,000. Did the cartoonist mean to suggest that the bank's board of directors was foolish? The purchase of the plane was part of Bert's employment contract with NBG, and that contract required two independent appraisers to set the plane's value. They did, and the bank paid the price they felt it was worth.

Nor did Bert misuse the airplane. That too was a figment of the press's imagination conditioned by government rules and expectations. His use was known and examined by the bank's directors and shareholders. It was their airplane, their pocketbook which paid for the trips. They never told Bert that he had misused it. They bought it so Bert could use it to attract business, and he did attract business—a lot of business—through personal appearances and travel facilitated by use of the plane.

After the long summer was over, Bert was able to put everything in perspective and even joke about it. On September 29, 1977, at a meeting of the Investment Association of New York, he told a couple of jokes that humorously indicate what we felt our predicament to be during that trying time:

A little lady went in to the meat market to buy a chicken for dinner. And the butcher said, "May I help you?"

And she said, "Yes, I'd like to buy a chicken."

And he said, "Well, do you see one in the case that you'd like to have?"

And she said, "Well, that one over there looks pretty good."

And he reached in there and pulled it out. And she said, "May I look at it?" She took it and she was holding it by the neck and she looked at it very carefully. She punched the breast to see how firm it was, and she pinched the thigh to see whether there was any color. She twisted the leg to see how strong it was and looked very carefully at the wings. She handed it back to the butcher and she said, "This won't do."

The butcher said, "Well, lady, of course, that's your prerogative and choice, but to tell you the honest-to-goodness truth, I doubt if you could pass that kind of test yourself."

A second story is told about the fellow who was walking through the zoo one day and he had looked at all the animals very closely and carefully. And all of a sudden he came upon the most unusual sight he had ever seen in his life. He looked in the lion's cage and saw a lamb lying there very peacefully at rest and he got very excited about it and turned to the zookeeper and said, "Well, at last the biblical prophecy has been fulfilled; a lion and a lamb are lying down together. I'm delighted to see that taking place."

But the zookeeper was amazed at the fellow's innocence and said, "Oh, no, you don't understand. You see, we put in a new lamb every day."

"Back during the last couple of months," Bert told the Investment Association audience, "I've been looking for that new lamb every day and he never showed up."

Unfortunately for us, the media did not find another lamb that summer. The trial by press continued. On September 9, Senator Percy suggested that Bert may have back-dated checks to take an improper tax deduction on his 1975 taxes. He did not ask Bert or our lawyers or accountant the reason for the dates on these checks. Nor did he check with the IRS to see when and how our taxes were paid. He didn't know that our taxes are paid quarterly and were automatically taken care of by our accountants. The reason for checks being out of order was obvious and simple—Bert had taken some checks out of his checkbook to carry with him. Senator Percy later apologized at the Senate hearings, but in a certain sense the damage was done. Some people were going to think that Bert was a tax cheat. All these untruths made public! All the harm we had to bear! False accusations leave their mark.

All my married life I've stood by Bert in good times and bad, and these were extraordinary circumstances. It was a public roasting where the victim is supposed to recant and crawl away blaming himself, simply to get the heat off. Bert stuck it out, and I stood by him. Have you ever been in a situation where you thought everybody in the room was looking at you? And you began to check to see if your dress was on straight, your slip showing or something? Do you know how uncomfortable and confused you can become? Well, the whole country was looking at us. And it took all the strength God could give us and all that prayer could do to keep us believing in ourselves and in what we knew to be true. When we cried, "Why us?" he gave us peace.

September was a month in which anyone in Washington who had an opinion about Bert—and in Washington almost everyone has an opinion—was asked for it. People who had absolutely no connection with his case and were not privy to information about it were appearing in the press saying Bert should or should not resign. Since bad new is good news as far as newspaper sales are concerned, there were more of the "should resign" opinions than "should not." But, I should explain to do Washington and politics a measure of justice, appearance is as powerful and important as substance. People were saying that even if Bert were totally innocent he would not be able to do his job when doubts lingered in some very influential people's minds. What worrried Bert most was the shadow that the public commotion had cast over President Carter. Bert's loyalty to the President and his goals was complete. He hated being the occasion and cause for the President's political opponents to question the President's credibility. For Bert it was a terrible dilemma—he was trapped between defending his name and honor, and casting a pall on the President he had pledged to serve.

We both longed for the case to be resolved. I trusted that the Senate hearings would be open and fair, thereby clearing Bert. I knew that, being the kind of man he was, his testimony would be strong and forthright. But there were so many details to worry about. If someone asked you to name names and give financial details about your business dealings five years ago—could you do it? Bert wanted to prepare in the best way he could and Clark Clifford and the other lawyers were helping him do that. All our personal financial records and transactions at the bank for the last decade were being compiled. Bert's defense would be based upon the facts and upon truth and not upon speculation, rumor and opinion.

The weekend before the hearings began, Bert and I went to Sea Island where he worked on writing his statement for three solid days. He'd write parts, read them to me, go back and rewrite and edit. Meanwhile the coffee cups kept being refilled, and I hovered around, offering suggestions, reviewing what he'd done, tidying up, making sandwiches. The lights burned late and we got little sleep.

At points during the second day it seemed to be an almost impossible task. How to defend oneself against a welter of charges and allegations ranging over almost ten years of business activity? How to explain with precision, clarity, honesty and in layman's language a multitude of technical business practices and banking strategies? And then how to condense it all into a reasonable time frame so it could be read and comprehended by the Senate and the viewing public. When darkness closed in around us on the second night, we were exhausted. I listened to the night noises from the marsh and almost wished I could fly away like a night bird on soundless wings.

But the morning of the last day dawned bright and cheerful, and we went back to work with a will—and everything fell into place and was formed into a strong, coherent argument. When Bert read the completed statement to me I knew it was right—not because of its detailed answers to the charges against him, but because his strength, decorum and basic honesty as a Christian businessman shone through. I was confident and ready to go back to Washington.

The family gathered the day before the hearing and spent the night at our townhouse or at nearby hotels. Barker and Rita and Mother and my stepfather came. Bert's sister and her husband came. Everyone was gathering around us. I was amazingly tranquil. Bert was ready, and he was confident.

At about 6:00 A.M. on the morning of September 15, Bert went over to the White House to have an early morning prayer session with the President. They read together special verses from Scripture and prayed for strength and that God's will be done. It was a fitting thing for two friends who had shared their faith, hopes and plans for the future in such prayer sessions since early years in the Georgia governor's office to spend this morning together.

Bert and I joined the family a little before 10:00 in the Senate Conference Room. Both boys were a blessing to me that day. David had graduated from Emory a year earlier, and since he had not yet married, he had been able to travel and stay with us more during this troubled period. Both David and Tram were following Bert's footsteps into banking. For the last year they had been working at the National Bank of Georgia. Each was calm, confident, steady. They sat on either side of me in that cold marble hearing room. My two fully-grown sons were like two strong pillars supporting me.

Then as millions watched on TV, Bert finally had his "day in court."

Just before Bert started to speak, I felt my breath coming short and fast. Would he be as nervous as I, facing the Senate and the whole nation? I knew he had nothing to fear, but would he quaver because of the stress of the situation? When I heard his strong deep voice begin to read I knew he was calm in spirit and that all would go well.

In Washington, effects are measured immediately. Letters and telegrams started pouring in to the White House, the Senate, to the Office of Management and Budget, praising Bert's defense and supporting him. And the letters just didn't stop.

When the committee adjourned for lunch, after Bert had read his statement, we took the whole family to the White House mess for lunch where we all could be served promptly and return in time to the hearing room.

The hearings went on all that afternoon and for two more days. There was tough questioning and Bert's restrained and detailed response. The media began to play another tune. Now they were talking about Bert as if he were a sports figure or boxer or a football player. He was "winning rounds" or "points." He was making a "goal line stand." He was "winning back his job." My head was spinning from all this. Where was the real Bert? Some reports painted him as a bad guy, others as a good guy. He was a villian, a hero, a star. But where was the Bert I knew—a decent man who was no better or worse than most others, who was trying to do a big job, raise his family, follow his conscience? Where was he?

We were fortunate, of course, to have defenders among disinterested and nonpartisan observers. Henry M. Wriston, President Emeritus of Brown University, wrote in *The New York Times* and *The Washington Post* some critical words about the process of the hearings. In part he said:

"The behavior of the Senate Governmental Affairs committee was scandalous. The chairman, Abraham A. Ribicoff, should be censured or dismissed from the Committee. He admitted he had done a negligent and superficial job at the confirmation hearings, and that alone should have precipitated his resignation, for failure to give adequate attention to his constitutional function.

"The senior minority member, Charles H. Percy, committed such a shocking trespass upon the rights of the 'defendant,' by suggesting that he had back-dated checks to improperly take an income tax deduction, that he had to apologize—a gesture wholly inadequate to the damage done. The least he should have done would have been to resign from the committee whose integrity he had besmirched.

"Both of these men participated in giving currency to the uncorroborated word of a convicted felon, a former vice president of Mr. Lance's Calhoun bank, who reportedly implicated Mr. Lance in embezzlement—which even superficial inquiry would have shown to be untrue. Yet on this unsubstantiated charge they sought a private meeting with President Carter. They went in the back door of the White House. They should have left by the basement."

Clark Clifford told me after the hearings that Bert had public opinion going his way. "How fickle public opinion is," I thought. I hoped that the nation and the world had caught a glimpse of the real Bert during the hearings—but I did not put my faith in television or the world's opinion. I trusted God to bring out of this whole twisted episode the good he wanted. His *opinion* and purpose were sure.

After the hearings our spirits soared; the public's response was heartwarming. But then came the news article about my brother Banks, and Bert's resignation on September 21. After the hubbub and the reporters in the street, it was nice to contemplate going home.

The day after he resigned, Bert and I planned our departure. We would go home to Calhoun for the weekend, but we wanted to do something special for the OMB staff and all our friends in Washington, so we sent out invitations to everybody—and I mean everybody—who worked in the White House or the Executive Office Building, including the telephone operators, custodians, the girls in the typing pool, everybody. We asked them all to come to a farewell party and let us say goodbye personally in Bert's office.

On Thursday we flew back to Calhoun and were met by crowds of people carrying signs welcoming us home. They took us by motorcade all the way downtown where we were officially greeted at the court house by two thousand people. How wonderful! This spontaneous outpouring of love from

old friends and neighbors. They released us from the hurt
and tension of Washington.

Then suddenly, that same night, we were faced with
another crisis!

Triumph and tragedy. While we were arriving in Calhoun on Thursday afternoon, September 22, Dr. Lance,
Bert's father, had fallen in his yard at home. At first it didn't
appear to be serious, but the next morning Bert's mother
called to tell us that he had been taken to the doctor for
X-rays and that his hip was broken. A pin needed to be put
in. We got ready to go right over to the hospital in Rome
where they had taken him to a specialist. We feared that
because of his age, 91, he might not survive the operation.
God diverts us from the petty to the truly important. Our
Washington crisis was painful, but it was not a life and death
situation. David backed the car out of the carport, we
jumped in, bought hamburgers along the way for lunch, and
then rushed to the hospital. We spent the rest of the day
there. Strangely, it was probably the one place where the
reporters would leave us alone. We spent the day quietly
among family and in prayer for Dr. Lance.

Bert's mother is in her mid-eighties, but she sat with us
the whole day. It was 7:30 that evening before they wheeled
Dr. Lance out of the recovery room. Thank God, he was
doing well. He had suffered a stroke about five years before
and had been in poor health for some time. We were afraid
that the hip operation would be too much for him.

On Sunday we went to church to give thanks for his
recovery and our return home—and we were doubly
blessed. As the service opened, the pastor announced that
he was canceling his sermon and was going to make this
Sunday "Bert and LaBelle Lance Praise the Lord Day."
Methodists are usually a fairly staid and unemotional church
people, but on that Sunday there was joy and tears as the
pastor ushered us to the pulpit. And there were more tears
when the congregation joined us in singing "How Great
Thou Art." Bert and I both took turns thanking the congregation for their welcome, their prayers, their strength, and
their love which had helped us through the difficult days of
summer. My eyes turned up to the stained glass windows in

whose light I had grown up, and filled with tears of joy. God gives us such beautiful moments to lift us up! I will remember that day as long as I live.

We returned to Washington that Sunday night and made last minute arrangements for the OMB reception on Monday. Our invitations had gone to just about everybody in government who had touched our lives, since we had come to Washington—Republicans as well as Democrats, and just scores and scores of others who had no official position, but were friends.

Well, everybody came! Including the President and Vice-President and their wives. Washington had rarely seen such a party. We served only punch and cookies, so that couldn't have been the reason for the heavy attendance. And it wasn't, in Washington's terms, a victory party. But hundreds and hundreds of people lined up through the corridors of the Executive Office Building all afternoon. Some of them waited nearly two hours just for the chance to step into Bert's office for a moment and shake hands and wish us well. They came because they liked Bert. I could hardly hold back the tears of happiness and surprise. Even the White House police took turns leaving their posts to attend. Most of the Cabinet officers and their wives were there, the leaders of the House and Senate, the Chief Justice and his wife, a dear friend, and members of the Supreme Court, the top members of the Federal Reserve Board, including Chairman Arthur Burns and Helen.

The thought occurred to me that if we had not passed through this awful time of trouble we'd never have known the depth and warmth of the affection and support so many hundreds of our friends demonstrated to us that day. The Lord was good. We were able to leave Washington with fond memories and go home in peace.

Returning home doesn't always end the story. Since we have become "news" we still seem to be followed, noticed, commented upon. If we go to a party, my gown is described and Bert's actions closely watched to provide "signs" for whatever the reporter is speculating about. If we don't go to certain parties, that too is noticed and the word is out that we are staying out of public view. Between Thanksgiving and Christmas we were still in the news, as one committee or another decided whether or not to continue going over the ground about Bert's management of the bank, our selling stock, etc.

Sometimes it was wearying. But whenever I'd get low, Bert would remind me of what we claimed from the beginning: if God gives you an opportunity, a job, a gift—whatever it is—you take it. You don't roll over, pull the covers up over your head and refuse it simply because the opportunity is not gift-wrapped with success. You grasp the chance, you lift the load, you do your share, you put in the talent God gave you to make this opportunity the success it can be. And you take the bad and make it as good as you can. You see the thing through to the end.

We were sustained. When there was trouble, we had the help of friends. If there were defeats, there were also successes. Bert lost one opportunity to serve, but gained another. In January the President asked both of us to serve as co-chairmen of the Friendship Force—America's people-to-people outreach to other nations. Rosalynn Carter is the very active honorary chairman. Now Bert's expertise and close association with the President and his understanding of the business community could be put to its most effective use. Bert also accepted an assignment as a news commentator on station WXIA-TV, an ABC affiliate in Atlanta.

Our schedule was suddenly jammed-packed with appointments, travel, missions again. Trips to Australia, France, Brussels and the Common Market, England, Italy, the Far East were planned. The resting time was over. We'd had a chance to recuperate. Now it was time to get back to work. For me it meant speaking, writing, extending the circle of my witness for the Lord. I want to be an Ambassador. My commission is the same as yours, coming from the same course, from the same *official* source: God.

CALHOUN, JANUARY 1978

I turned right at the little combination gas station and store, going north out of town and headed toward Lancelot.

I drove through the gates decorated with federal eagles and up past the chapel we had built by the pond and stopped at Bert's office, which we call Eagle's Nest.

Lancelot has grown just as we have grown. We started with thirty-three acres—an old pig farm. We added adjacent property until we have over three hundred acres. It's rocky land. We say it grows stones, because after every rain more appear as the soil washes away. We love it.

I peeked in his office to see if Bert was all right. He was working at his desk, sitting in the chair that had been his as a Cabinet Officer. (Each man who serves there is given his chair when he leaves office.) On the walls American and Georgian flags were hung. He looked up and waved and went back to his work. He was speaking, often now, sometimes several times a week, on economic and governmental themes. His roles in government almost seemed to be expanding since he left the OMB. He was still visiting and conferring with the President every week. Sharing his opinions, and those he hears from people outside of government about the economy, the Panama Canal, the Mideast and a hundred other topics.

And now he and I were being asked to travel the world as heads of America's new mission to the world to convey our honesty of purpose and intention for peace to people everywhere. The world had become our parish.

It was more than I could have imagined when leaving Washington a few months ago. I wondered if I would be adequate to the task. I trusted that if God wanted me for it, he would make me suitable for the work. But it was such a big responsibility. I worried about it. I wondered where our lives were headed now.

I decided to go for a walk. I walked further up the hill. The day was bright and cold. The whole eastern seaboard had been engulfed by storms and a cold wave. All the leaves were long off the hardwoods, but the pine trees and evergreens still gave some of the fragrance of Christmas to the frosty air.

My mind began to clear, as I walked up the slope, avoiding the frozen spots and rocks. Seasons change and leaves fall, then birds arrive, I thought. Babies are born and old folks die, life changes. No two days are the same. Through a strength beyond sorrow and pain, through the joys and strength of God, we endure. We learn to let go of our children, homes, jobs—we learn to abide and to accept our roles and tasks and burdens and go on climb upward. Sorrow will pass, pain, trouble, earthly travail—all will be transformed in Christ. Each person must die to himself to be reborn in Christ. Even this solid earth will some day be transformed by his Second Coming.

God alone could make this plan perfect—the earth in all its variety, complexity and unity reflects it. Everything from the orderliness of nature to the orderliness of our minds is a model of his perfect plan. It is that we are blinded by sin, and we must struggle to see the light. Daily crises will occur— family problems, sorrows, heartbreak—but with God's help we shall overcome them.

I reached the crest of the hill above Eagle's Nest and turned around to survey the countryside that I love: the land that held all my childhood memories, the home of my family and friends, the place where I learned my ABC's, had my first date, bore my first child, felt my first pangs of mortality in the death of loved ones.

My spirit surged with joy. The result of this last dramatic year seemed a loss, a failure, viewed from the perspective of human values. But if I attempted to see it all through the eyes of God, its secret worth and meaning began to emerge. God uses everything to bring about faith. He uses every- thing to witness to his glory. He would use me and all the events of my life in this way, and I prayed only that I could be better able to see it and to understand.

Someday, if we only believe, we will be changed in the twinkling of an eye into one of God's heavenly beings. For now, we live in his embrace; we are alive for this moment to honor him, and soon we will sing his glory for eternity.